To: Ba...
May G...

B.S.Cross/.

My Friends
Love

The RELEVANCE *of* CHRISTIAN COUNSELING TODAY

The RELEVANCE *of* CHRISTIAN COUNSELING TODAY

A Practical Beginners Guide to 21 Century Pastoral Counseling

Beverly Sterling-Cross

Xulon Press

Xulon Press
2301 Lucien Way #415
Maitland, FL 32751
407.339.4217
www.xulonpress.com

© 2018 by Beverly Sterling-Cross

All rights reserved solely by the author. The author guarantees all contents are original and do not infringe upon the legal rights of any other person or work. No part of this book may be reproduced in any form without the permission of the author. The views expressed in this book are not necessarily those of the publisher.

Unless otherwise indicated, Scripture quotations taken from the King James Version (KJV) – public domain.

Printed in the United States of America.

ISBN-13: 9781545650905

DEDICATION

$\mathcal{J}$t is with much love and appreciation that I dedicate this book to my loving and supportive husband Dolphy. We have become a team and partners in ministry. With his wisdom and guidance, we were able to create "Cross' Basement Theory for Couples Conflict Resolution." This diagnostic instrument will prove to be an invaluable tool for counseling couples in conflict and for use in general Couples Therapy.

ABSTRACT

*T*he world has changed significantly and it will continue to change because people are in a constant state of metamorphosis. This change impacts the way people live and interrelate on a daily basis and manifest itself in private and public places including churches. I am studying the relevance of Christian counseling today. This study is based on my general observations and will be limited to only those who practice the Christian Faith. It is my desire to find out, who are sitting in the pews each week in churches. I am trying to discover if their felt needs are being met especially from the pulpit. The Christian churches in general and the pastors in particular are preparing their members to go to heaven while overlooking the reality of living successfully on earth. The scripture teaches that we are to occupy until Jesus comes (Luke 19:13). Therefore, I believe that Christians should be prepared to live successfully on earth until death or translation comes. Success here does not necessarily mean money but more so building relationship. In order to arrive at a logical outcome in a qualitative manner, I will pull together from the many sources that make up my literature review to show that the people sitting in the pews of churches every week share many of the mental and social problems that non-committed people face every day. Church members are also plagued with divorce, depression, anger, resentment, drug abuse, infidelity, domestic violence, grief, addictions, mental health issues, and general sickness. These constitute a large part of the stresses of life but are not given priority from the pulpit. The findings will be very revealing because people need to know and understand that the people who go to church are ordinary people who are affected by the cares and stresses of life, while seeking a better life. Some families are mentally and socially fractured, others are broken and need help in healing towards personal wholeness. Cross' Basement Theory is a conflict resolution instrument that I have developed and tested on twelve couples with the same positive results. These couples signed an informed consent that told them that their names would not be disclosed to any other person and the information would be used solely for the purpose of verifying the accuracy of the Basement Theory. The instrument will be fully explained in this thesis. The significance of this thesis will impact pastors and those who have embraced the discipline of Christian counseling. It will help to sensitize them to know that a change in the content and context of their preaching is needed. A church, rightly understood, should be a place where members and non-members can go to receive education, counsel, and resources to deal with the daily challenges of life. Sometimes the entire congregation will have to be transformed into a large therapy class because of the level of brokenness in the lives of parishioners. Ultimately, the result showed that Christian counseling was still very relevant in a Christian church, culture, and society.

FOREWORD

I am delighted to hear that Mrs. Beverly Sterling-Cross has completed the requirements and has obtained a doctorate in Christian counseling. She is eminently qualified both by her background and temperament to serve as a Christian counselor. Mrs. Cross has been an ardent and faithful Christian for all her life and is not only aware of Christian tenets but has lived them. She is truly a committed Christian.

Beverly's sterling traits of character also equip her to serve as a beacon of hope to anyone requiring the help of a Christian counselor. She is a people person and has a gregarious personality. She carries a very infectious smile and is a very warm, kind, and thoughtful person. This book on the Relevance of Christian Counseling Today is well written and will undoubtedly prove to be an invaluable resource for her target audience as well as the layperson in the pews.

Beverly has my wholehearted congratulations and heartfelt commendations on a job well done. I eagerly anticipate the day when she teams up with her husband, Dr. Dolphy Cross to provide a much-needed counseling service to pastoral families and the general community for the honor and glory of God.

Sincerely,
Dr. Louis R. Browne, Ph.D.
Professor of Anatomy and Physiology, (Ret.)

Acknowledgements

It is with a deep sense of gratitude and thankfulness that I acknowledge the persons whose encouragement and support helped to make this book possible.

I thank Dr. Frank Moore for his guidance and words of encouragement throughout the entire research and writing process. His positive and reassuring comments gave me the needed courage to turn this dissertation into a book to share with others. I will forever be indebted to my loving husband, Dr. Dolphy Cross who convinced me that I am a natural counselor and whose idea it was to include in this book, the Basement Theory for Couples Conflict Resolution to which I have attributed our surname. I wish to thank Dr. Louis Browne who wrote the foreword and was very kind in his remarks. I furthermore, acknowledge Dr. Shaton

Monique Glover-Alves and Dr. James Hamilton who proofread the rough draft and gave helpful suggestions.

Lastly, but in no way least, I must thank my two sons, Dr. Milton Sterling and Wesley Sterling as well as my daughter-in-law Kyna for believing in me and who were my cheerleaders throughout the process. Their insightful suggestions and encouragements gave me the added impetus to complete this project. I pray that God's blessings will rest upon all those who contributed to the success of this project and may it be a blessing to all who turn its pages to read.

TABLE OF CONTENTS

INTRODUCTION

This world is in a moral decline and relationships at every level have felt the impact of this moral decadence. All evidences seem to suggest that there is no counter force to stem the downward spiral of human behavior. The scripture teaches that as it gets closer to the end of the world, man will become lovers of pleasure more than lovers of God, and in the process their hearts will fail them for fear (2Tim.3:4, Lk.21:26). Man must change but he cannot do this by himself. Any real change must include God who seeks to communicate to man through His written word. This is the essence of Christian counseling and according to Jay Adams (1979) the Bible is the basis for Christian counseling and Christian counseling is about changing lives by changing values, beliefs, attitudes, relationships, and behaviors.

There is a growing need for more Christian counselors today who will make the pursuits of the fruits of the spirit top priority (Gal. 5:22-23). There must be a change, and the church where people meet weekly can be a tremendous vehicle to initiate this change, especially from sinful habits and addictive behaviors. Jesus is still the only answer to man's sinful dilemma and the Bible is still the inspired, authoritative, and infallible word of God.

Sinful man cannot change himself, especially from bad lifestyle habits to good. According to Carol DiClemente (2003) the dynamic and multidimensional change perspective offers an interactive framework for understanding change and the problem of addiction and recovery. Christian counselors must understand these dimensions of change which are: stages of change, processes of change, markers of change, and context of change. These clearly delineated changes will assist the Christian counselor and other practitioners to identify patterns of behavior that can be labelled addictive behavior and consequently provide the vehicle toward corrective treatment interventions. Since the church is considered a place for healing, this healing must not be confined to the spiritual, but also extend to the mental, physical, and social aspects of the human experience. We must therefore, find answers to the following questions: (1) are Christian churches today deliberate and purposefully planning to meet the mental, physical, and social needs of people in the pews? (2) are pastors preparing academically and professionally to address these growing concerns and needs from the pulpit?

Family problems are not disjointed, they are all interrelated and have a starting point. What affects the parents affects the children and sometimes problems among siblings can spawn marital problems between parents. Cross' Basement Theory for Couples Conflict Resolution (CBTCCR) has proven to be a tremendous diagnostic instrument to help couples in conflict to deal with the main issue and root cause of conflict. It also helps in providing a solid counseling platform for pre-marital counseling.

CHAPTER 1

WHAT IS MISSING FROM THE TWENTY-FIRST CENTURY PULPIT

amilies today are plagued with many different problems that affect people of all ages. A well trained and alert Christian counselor, especially a clergy person, should be able to identify and provide needed professional help for many of these families. Domestic violence, addiction, and suicide are among those that stand out and are more prevalent. Christian counselors are needed more today because as population increases so do our problems and Christians are not immune to the aforementioned problems.

People are angry and this anger has manifested itself in the sharp increase in domestic violence, school

violence, and the steady increase in church related violence. There must be a change and the church where
people meet weekly can be a tremendous vehicle to
initiate this change, especially from sinful habits and
addictive behaviors. The questions that the Christian
culture faces today are: are preachers declaring from
their pulpits the dangers of sinful habits, tendencies,
and behaviors? Is the gospel aimed at making people
feel good about themselves or making them aware of
sinful lifestyle and the plan of salvation?

The Gospel is Good News and any good news
should make the people who hear it feel happy. God is
the Provider who provides for his children. However,
today's Prosperity preaching from the pulpit should not
be categorized as Gospel which is Good News! The
prosperity preaching today has its place and time but it
should not occupy the center of the Gospel. This type of
preaching serves the purpose of meeting the demands
of itching ears (2Tim. 4:2-4), because it instills some
hope and leaves the listener feeling good.

All Bible students know fully well that while the
Gospel is Good News, it does not necessarily leave all
the hearers happy and hopeful. The rich young ruler
heard the saving gospel from Jesus and he was not

happy nor hopeful (Mk.10:18-22, Lk.18:18-23). King Agrippa, Felix, and Festus heard the testimony from St. Paul (Acts. 26:27, 28; 24:24, 25; 25). These men heard the saving power of the Gospel Good News, but they were not happy and all the historical evidences point to the fact that they never did accept Christ a Lord and Savior.

There are people who will be lost in church because they are not being prepared from the pulpit for heaven. There is a spiritual ingredient that is missing from the twenty-first century pulpit. This missing ingredient is inextricably bound to the mental and the social aspects of mankind that cannot be addressed by simply preaching that we should love one another. There is a need for more pastors to be equipped with the knowledge of Christian counseling because they already have the spiritual component that is needed for compassionate care. Everything that happens in the community, the nation, and the world ultimately impacts the church. Unfortunately, the church is overlooked because such need is not supposed to be inherent in a Christian congregation.

Christian counseling is a caring profession and the increase in mental health cases shows that the church is not excluded. Pastors should therefore, seek to become members of such professional organization after equipping themselves with the basic knowledge. Pastors already have the spiritual qualification for Christian counseling. Clinton (2009) suggests that such a person should have some level of spirituality in order to exhibit compassionate empathy. Clinton further states that, sitting in the pews of every church are people who are touched by addiction, divorce, violence, depression, grief, confusion, loneliness, and a thousand other evidences of living as broken people in a fallen world.

Life is all about relationships, the vertical relationship between man and God and the horizontal relationship between man and his fellowmen. Ronald Richardson (2010) infers that effective counseling is built on a relationship of trust between the client and the counselor. Broken people in a fallen world who are striving to have a good and understanding relationship will find it illusive. They will instead run into misunderstandings, which in turn lead to conflicts and ultimately division and separation. This inevitable end result can be avoided or significantly reduced if the pastors begin to prepare themselves now to meet the challenge.

As I strive to answer the question of what is missing from the twenty-first century pulpit, I have come to realize that the answer to this problematic question is found both in the pulpit and the pews. According to Larry Crabb (1977) every Christian is called to a ministry of helping and encouraging others, especially those in the household of faith. Crabb further states that the major concern is to encourage as many as possible to be specifically trained for a specialized ministry of counseling involving a deeper exploration into stubborn problems (Crabb, 1977). To this end, Randolph Sanders (1984) asserts that, the Christian counselor should strive for scholarship, professional competence, and integrity. In order for the Christian therapist to excel professionally and spiritually, Sanders (1984) further states that it is essential to identify, understand and apply appropriate guidelines and limits to the service being provided.

EVANGELIST OR SHEPHERD

Most pastors very early in their ministries strive to become evangelists, especially among evangelicals and those of the Caribbean and African American cultures. An evangelist in this context means someone who conducts evangelistic series nationally or internationally. These series would run from two to eight weeks, with evangelistic type preaching five nights each week. While some of these evangelists are itinerant and go from city to city preaching the gospel, many of them are pastors with one and two local congregations. Most pastors strive to become evangelists because the denomination to which they belong equates baptisms as proof of their calling to ministry or use it as a measuring rod that pastoral work is being done.

The purpose for each evangelistic series is to win and baptize souls for Christ. Interestingly however, most times this is done at the expense of those who have already been won but lacks the nurturing for strength and stability. This results in a revolving door experience in which the souls that are won and baptized, enters the church through the front door but shortly thereafter, leaves through the invisible back door. This will continue in any congregation or church that places the winning and baptizing of souls above the nurturing of those already won.

All shepherds are pastors but not all pastors can be shepherds. A shepherd is a sheep herder, one who takes care of the needs of the flock. Jesus sets the example of the perfect shepherd (Psalm 23). Shepherds cannot produce sheep only sheep can produce sheep. Therefore, the smart shepherd takes time to care for the sheep and nurtures the sheep to become productive. The essence of church growth in not so much in evangelistic exploits but in compassionate caring and practical loving and nurturing of the sheep. Every pastor therefore, should strive to become competent in Christian counseling in order to fill one of the main voids in the twenty-first century pulpit. Felt needs in the pews must first be met from the pulpit and complemented through seminars and workshops.

FROM THE CRADLE TO THE GRAVE

Just as a shepherd is expected to take care of the lambs to the aging sheep, the pastor must be able to nurture his members from the cradle to the grave. The pastor has a special role to play as the spiritual leader of his or her congregation. The pastor must be equipped to provide support and even care to parishioners with life threatening illnesses. The pastor, the shepherd of the flock, should be able to help someone to reclaim their spirituality as a source of healing and empowerment and thereby develop a renewed sense of hope and a more realistic and balanced view of the world (Rogers & Knoenig, 2002).

People who are afflicted with heart disease, cancer, alzheimer's, and any other type of illness, need to know that the pastor cares. The pastor is in a unique position of trust and should be able to give support and compassionate care. Sometimes the ministry of presence is needed more than counsel. There are times when no spoken word is needed and if communication is pressed upon the grieving, it can do more harm than good. When illness sets in both the sick as well as the family caregiver can experience anger. Most time this type of anger is bottled up by the patient and the family member who is also spouse and caregiver. This anger however, will not stay bottled up indefinitely.

It is important for a pastor to encourage appropriate expression of anger to assist the individuals in this endeavor. Sometimes pastors may find that they are the object of displaced anger." (Rogers & Knoenig, 2002). The caring shepherd will know that this displaced anger should not be taken personal but can instead be used to lay the foundation for prayer, meditation, and other healing practices. This is one of the rolls of a caring pastor who knows what it means to be a shepherd of the flock. In order for healing to take place, the individual must be purged of anger.

ALZHEIMER'S

In 1906, Alois Alzheimer (a German physician) described the disease that now bears his name. He treated a patient in her early fifties who exhibited behavioral symptoms normally present in older people. When an autopsy was performed, numerous tangles and plaques were discovered in the brain, and these have become characteristic of the illness (Otwell, 2007). According to Jacob Silverman, Alzheimer's disease is a neurodegenerative disease and the most prevalent form of Dementia. It has no cure and it is always fatal. (health.howstuffworks.com/mental-health/neurological-conditions/alzheimers.htm). Alzheimer's disease affects the brain and it progresses through three stages, early, moderate, and severe. This is important in pastoral ministry because the pastor as a shepherd should know how to minister to a parishioner with alzheimer's. Sadly however, very few pastors know how to minister and provide care at this level.

One thing is clear to those who study the disease, Alzheimer is recognized as an illness and not a consequence of aging (Otwell, 2007). It was the general believed that all elderly people would eventually become senile, if they live long enough. However, we know today that people can live for well over one hundred years without becoming senile. We owe a debt of gratitude to Lois Alzheimer and others for uncovering the disease. Alzheimer's patients need spiritual comfort just like any other person, but the cry from pastors is that they really don't know how to minister to these people. Alzheimer's patients and their families are spiritual beings and have spiritual needs even though they may be unaware of them or not feel comfortable sharing them (Otwell, 2007).

The inability to minister effectively to a person or a parishioner with alzheimer's is one of the many things that is missing from the twenty-first century pulpit. Not being able to minister to the sick person with Alzheimer's is very sad. If the pastor's knowledge and skillset does not allow him or her to minister to the member with Alzheimer's, how can spiritual care be extended to the family members? The pastor who cannot minister to the Alzheimer's patient will also have little or no understanding of what the family members as caregivers are going through. This level of ministry should never be taken for granted and it is one that certainly needs more attention.

It is very important for the pastor to acquire some level of professional training that will alert him or her to the signs and symptoms of the onset of certain disease like alzheimer's. This knowledge can help the caring pastor to alert and even prepare a spouse and family members to prepare for the inevitable. The compassionate and caring pastor should know that preaching is just one part of ministry. Parishioners, in times of need, often turn to their clergyperson (Otwell, 2007). The clergyperson has a unique opportunity to help alzheimer's patients and their families because of their knowledge of community resources and their faith and ability in sharing God's love.

There is no one person with all the answers, but there are some basic answers that a caring pastor should have to share with patient and family members with diagnosed Alzheimer's disease. The pastor should be able to recommend support groups to the family which can be a powerful avenue for mutual help. The pastor should have information on local, state, and federal resources to assist Alzheimer's patients and their families. The very diagnosis brings with it a fountain of stress, worry, and anxiety both for the patient and family. A caring and well-informed clergyperson can do much to alleviate much of the stress and fear.

It is dangerous for any clergyperson without some form of specialized training to attempt counseling with a patient with Alzheimer's or early stage dementia. Yale (2013) asserts that due to the highly specialized and sensitive nature of the intervention, it is mandated that the practitioners have solid credentials, adequate experience, and relevant personal attributes. It is also of equal importance and essential for the clergyperson to have some mental health experience and some skill in working with people with dementia (Yale, 2013). Being a pastoral counselor does not qualify one to counsel people with Alzheimer's. Well credentialed counselors without dementia experience will not be well versed in the unique emotional, practical, and lifestyle challenges facing people with early stage dementia.

SICKNESS AND DEATH

Sickness and death in a family introduce a different phase in pastoral ministry that can no longer be ignored or avoided. While the pastor's denomination may not require any special training for their pastors in this area, it is incumbent on the pastor to become proficient in all areas of pastoral ministry. Sickness and death enter the world as a consequence of sin. God warned Adam that disobedience to His command would result in death (Gen. 2:17), and the scripture further teaches that the wages of sin is death (Rom. 6:23). The caring pastor can do much to bring about peace, comfort, and assurance to the sick, as well as the bereaved ones at the time of death.

The caring pastor must know how and when to shift roles from shepherd to servant and from counselor to comforter. As the pastor seeks to play these different roles he or she must understand that it is imperative that their own lives be in tandem with the Spirit through reading of the scripture and prayer. All Christian counseling is being called to an empirical accountability and the pastor in the local pulpit should be no exception (Clinton, et al., 2005).

The Bible is the basis for Christian counseling and Christian counseling is about changing lives by changing values, beliefs, attitudes, relationships, and behaviors (Adams, 1997). I believe that life in general is all about relationships. The vertical relationship between man and God, and the horizontal relationship between man and his fellowmen. In order for the pastor to be effective he or she must have an active relationship with God through prayer and the study of the scripture. A pastor cannot be an effective counselor if he or she only has a grade school knowledge of the Bible. The Bible must become the preacher's manual, resource book, and overall guide.

According to Adams (1997), the counselor's ability to use the scripture in counseling should never be called into question. The counselor must be converted and is able to demonstrate that there is biblical authority for the directions he or she gives a counselee. When sickness and death set in, your personal thoughts and feeling must give way to what the word of God says.

Scriptures aptly chosen can be a powerful source of comfort to any believer who is experiencing pain. God speaks to man through the scripture, the scripture is the word of God and it comes from God (1Tim. 3:16).

Bible students understand the nature of God to be omnipotent, omnipresence, omniscience, and immutable. Man cannot escape God, neither can he escape God's love and mercy. A counselee can no more avoid and ignore God than he or she can live without air, God is his atmosphere. The Bible teaches that while we were yet sinners, Christ died for us (Rom. 5:8). This means that while we were living in defeat, without any hope, God sent His Son to die for us. We, without a doubt should trust God to save us because he has proven his love for us without condition or reservation. We can and should trust God to save us, because He has proven His love for us (John 3:16).

God wants us to be in constant communication with Him and prayer is that vehicle that is made available to us to communicate with God. It makes much sense therefore, for counselees and all Christians to learn to pray and to listen to God in return. Sickness and death bring about those times when people are willing to listen to the still small voice of the Spirit. Man needs to have a relationship with God, and this relationship can only be developed through communication. Prayer is the main medium through which man communicates with God. God in turn communicates with man through other intermediaries like the written word, nature, and ultimately, through the life of Christ.

It is clear that humanistic philosophy and teachings have pose a problem for Christian counselors because humanism puts human being in the place of God. General counselors seek to help human beings to change by focusing on human beings themselves. The problem from my perspective is, without God no genuine or lasting change can take place. When Adam and Eve sinned, they had fallen so far that the image of God in them was almost obliterated and needed to be renewed (James 3:9, Eph. 4:23). Sinful man cannot do anything good without a selfish agenda and ulterior motive. Sinful man certainly cannot by doing good, change his sinful nature. There can be no change without regeneration through divine intervention.

Regeneration brings with it a new capacity for knowing and for doing God's will. Like Adam, we are social and gregarious beings, we have a wide capacity for fellowship (Adams, 1997). In my opinion, the devil

seeks to capitalize on sickness and death in our experiences to use them to weaken us spiritually and ultimately cut us off from God. The pastoral counselor
can also use sickness and death in a positive way to
reveal God's mercy and love even in suffering and
death. Death is not the end for the Christian who
embraces Jesus as the Savior therefore, death should
not bring on fear.

GRIEF AND BEREAVEMENT COUNSELING

Every human being from birth experiences some
form of grief in life. Grief is not limited to any special culture, nationality, socio-economic background,
or skin color. According to Neimeyer (2012), grief is
a state that encompasses many emotions; sadness and
longing, certainty, but also rage, guilt and fear. Since
this holds true as it relates to human behavior in grief
and bereavement, then its all the more reason for pastors to improve on their pastoral counseling knowledge
with the complementing skills of grief and bereavement counseling.

Trauma can also bring pain and grief. It may very
well be accepted as a natural part of life because every

individual is born into a life of trauma. Trauma begins for an individual from the time the umbilical cord is severed and the baby has to breath on its own for the very first time (Neimeyer, 2012). Grief is real and can last a very long time. If proper intervention is not administered to help the client to manage painful emotions, thoughts, and memories associate with the irreversibility of separation, such a person can experience Prolonged Grief Disorder (Neimeyer, 2012).

Anyone who believes in the authenticity of scripture will agree that sin by virtue of its nature, is traumatic. The scripture teaches that man was born in sin and shapes in inequity and all have sinned and come short of the glory of God (Rom. 3:23). Grief then, is an inescapable occurrence that may occurs several times in a person's life. Every pastor in general and pastoral counselors in particular should strive to understand grief and to recognize the role it plays in medical and psychiatric problems.

The knowledge in grief counseling will help the pastoral counselor to know when and where his or her skillset stops. More importantly, the pastoral counselor should know when to refer the individual or parishioner for further help. It is quite clear that pastoral counselors need to acquire techniques for grief counseling and learn how to apply creative practices for counseling the bereaved. Special training is needed and it is available for those who are interested in grief counseling. Neimeyer (2012) suggests that behavioral experiments should be applied in congruent fashion with the client being aware of their rationale and being motivated to engage in them. However, cognitive restructuring is one of the central interventions, apart from exposure and behavioral activations.

Every grieving person and mourner must get to the place where they can permit self to be healthy. If the mourner cannot permit self to be healthy, no treatment in the world will make a difference until that mourner decides it is permissible to let it go (Neimeyer, 2012). It is the responsibility of the therapist to listen acutely for any overt statement. Overt statements may be designed to be spoken directly to the relevant person. The purpose of an overt statement is to induce an emotional deepening in any specific area selected by the therapist. Here highly personal phrases are used by the client in expressing key material that may have already emerge in less direct form (Neimeyer, 2012).

Life is made up of choices and even the grieving individual has to make a choice. Neimeyer (2012) clearly states that it is important for the therapist to highlight that the client has a choice rather than directing the client to make a specific choice. The idea that the client can choose his or her attitude might be viewed as a cognitive reframing strategy. Direct journaling can be used to facilitate meaning and disruptive life stories can become their effective self-narrative. It is the responsibility of the pastoral counselor to make the suggestion or recommendation that the grieving person grieve freely while providing options to overcome.

Journaling can be very effective especially for family. Metaphors can also be used as meaning-making symbols in treating trauma and grief while spirituality and religion continue to be indispensable to many who have a religious faith (Neimeyer, 2012). Art therapy plays its part especially with those who find it difficult to express themselves verbally. Art therapy can lead to opening up the photo album and recapturing pleasant memories. Different people will respond differently to some therapies and interventions, one shoe does not fit all. Therefore, a basic knowledge of the different types of therapies would be a plus for any pastor who engages in counseling.

Learning the art of grief counseling is not beyond the scope of the pastor. In fact, it is highly recommended that a pastor acquires the skill and technique in grief counseling because grief is one of life's realities that is inevitable. One of the first rules is the self-care of the pastor or the therapist. A pastor's wellbeing and ability to be receptive and attuned are two edges of the same self-care process of staying open to and in touch with one self in experiencing the pain of the client. Taking care of oneself is built into the process of being present (Neimeyer, 2012).

GRIEF AS PHYSICAL ILLNESS OR DISEASE

Grief has been compared to physical illness. In the Old Testament, the prophet Isaiah admonishes to "bind up the broken hearted," giving the impression that severe grief can somehow damage the heart. Both grief and physical illness take time for healing and, indeed, both of them include emotional and physical aspects (Worden, 1991). In comparing physical illness and grief, Bertha Simos states that, "both may be self-limiting or require intervention by others, and in both, recovery can range from a complete return to the pre-existing state of health and well-being, to partial recovery, to improved growth and productivity, or both can inflict permanent damage, progressive decline or even death (Simos, 1979). Rightly understood, this could change even the way men and women are prepared and trained for ministry in the seminaries of the world. The question that is left to be answered now is, is grief a form of disease?

According to Worden (1991) Psychiatrist George Engel raised the interesting question, "is grief a disease?" in a thought provoking essay published in Psychosomatic Medicine. Engel's thesis is that the loss of a loved one is psychologically traumatic. He argues that grief represents a departure from the state of health and well-being, and just as healing is necessary in the psychological realm in order to bring into homeostatic balance, a period of time is likewise needed to return the mourner to a similar state of equilibrium. I would be more comfortable to say that grief is like disease.

Engel's argument makes so much sense and strengthens my resolve that there must be a paradigm shift in the way pastor are trained and prepared for ministry. Pastors are in the healing business and Engel sees mourning as a course that takes time until restoration of function can take place because the process of mourning is similar to the process of healing (Worden, 1992). Healing cannot occur until mourning is complete. Mourning and grief therefore, should be encouraged. There is no timeline to the end of grief and mourning, this is based on the individual.

The growing concern on my part is that most pastors who should be shepherds of their flocks are clueless as to what most people experience following a loss. Many have little or no understanding of the four main tasks of mourning, how to know when grief is finished, how to identify complicated grief and how to treat it. More importantly, pastors need to know how to help families in the resolution of a loss and they must strive to maximize their effectiveness as pastoral counselors. The pain of grief can be long lasting and excruciating. When people who do not understand surround the grieving person and make certain comments regarding their prolonged grief, it can make the pain of grief worse.

Every pastor is confronted with issues relating to grief sometimes on a daily basis. Majority of the pastors whose skillsets are limited in this area, resort to prayer, which of course is a powerful intervention but sometimes complicated grief will need aggressive psychological intervention associated with prayer. Common sense would dictate that a Christian with a broken arm or leg would seek medical attention to reset the broken bone while praying that surgery would be free from complications and the healing complete and whole. Grief is like physical illness.

There are normal manifestations of grief such as feelings of: sadness, anger, guilt and self-reproach, anxiety, loneliness, fatigue, helplessness, shock, emancipation, relief, and numbness. There is a thin line between grief and depression. Worden (1991) states that, "it is true that grief looks very much like depression and is also true that grieving may develop into full-blown depression." Worden (1991) further asserts that, "one of the functions of the counselor who has contact with people during time of acute grief is to assess which patients might be undergoing the development of a major depression." Grief can be an immediate or delayed experience that can be brief or it can go on for very long time.

It is important that a diagnosis be made before an intervention or treatment is administered. This call for training and professional know how that a regular clergy person does not possess. There are a number of clues to an unresolved grief reaction (Worden, 1991). Lazare (1979) has given an excellent taxonomy of twelve clues to identify unresolved grief, six of which will be listed as follows: (1) the person cannot speak of the deceased without experiencing intense and fresh grief, (2) some relatively minor event triggers off an intense grief reaction, (3) theme of loss come up in a clinical interview, (4) unwillingness to move material possession belonging to the deceased, (5) matching physical symptoms revealed upon medical examination, (6) unaccountable sadness occurring at a certain time each year.

This information should not be confined to the professional therapist. This is information for the pastoral counselor. It is interesting to note that the goal of grief therapy is somewhat different from the goal of grief counseling (Worden, 1991). Most pastors are not therapists, they are mostly counselors. Therefore, with this knowledge of being able to make a reasonable diagnosis, the pastoral counselor can make an intelligent referral to a grief therapist so that his or her parishioner or client can get the needed help in a timely manner.

According to Worden (1991), the goal of grief therapy is to resolve the conflicts of separation and to facilitate the completion of the grief tasks. It is important for the counselor or therapist to ask certain questions. One such question should be, what item have you save after the death of your loved one? Some will keep letters, clothe, etc. Saying goodbye does not mean you forget the person, it helps to prepares the individual to go on with life. Gestalt therapy can also be used in which the empty chair is introduced as the individual speaks to the deceased in the present tense (Warden, 1991). If this approach is used it must be used towards closure and not for ongoing therapy. The chair will always be empty and there is no one sitting there and no communication can take place with the deceased.

The Christian community has a faith foundation that can help them to overcome grief. Faith can facilitate an ordering and re-ordering of emotional experiences that initially feel random and cruel, transforming them into something that, at least from God's vantage point, has divine purpose and eternal meaning

(Neimeyer, 2012). The ministry of presence and prayer are very important interventions for a person of faith at the time of a loss. According to Neimeyer (2012) for many believers, faith sustains them through what can be one of life's darkest moments. Most human beings frequently strive to make sense of loss and subsequent grief through spirituality or religion.

Special types of losses create distinct problems for the survivors. Such losses include but not limited to: suicide, sudden death, sudden infant death, miscarriage and still birth, abortion, anticipated death, and aids. The pastor must help the survivors to deal with anger, guilt, blame, and the reality test of abandonment. Anticipatory grief can be like a cushion as it provides the survivor with the forewarning to begin the task of mourning. The reality is, outside of the hospice organization with their interdisciplinary team's intervention, which includes the chaplain's visit, most families whose sick stays home, are not exposed or introduced to anticipatory grief. Here again is the need for a paradigm shift in the way pastors are prepared for ministry.

Families are hurting in many different ways and children are made to suffer because of the loss of parents and siblings. The family bond has been broken and the attachment severed. Few can overcome this scar without spiritual and professional interventions. This is when the understanding of attachment becomes important because children who have lost their parents in childhood or adolescence are susceptible to depression (Worden, 1991). Sometimes ongoing counseling is needed where children are concerned, especially those of early teen age. The lack of knowledge in this area of ministry has resulted in a high level of insensitivity toward the hurting people.

The meaning of attachment is fundamental to one's understanding of the impact of a loss and the human behavior associated with such loss. Worden (1991) extracted from Bowlby's attachment theory that included data from ethology, control theory, cognitive psychology, neurophysiology, and developmental biology to show the strong affectional bonds that can exist between and among people. He shows the strong emotional reaction that occurs when those bonds are threatens or broken. People need people because we are gregarious beings, we like company. Celibacy was never God's plan for the human family, we need each other for praise, fellowship, and for comfort in times of sadness and loss.

Mourning is necessary if the individual mourner is to maintain equilibrium. Worden (1991) suggests, that there are four tasks of mourning which are: (1) to accept the reality of the loss, (2) to work through the pain of grief, (3) to adjust to an environment in which the deceased is missing, and (4) to emotionally relocate the deceased and move on with life. These four things will not occur the same time. In fact, no one can put a time limit as to when these will be accomplished but a person can know when it is over. Worden (1991) suggests that mourning can be considered finish when a person can reinvest his or her emotions back into life and living. A completed grief is when the person is able to think of the deceased without pain. Grief can be exaggerated and the person resort to maladaptive behavior and it can also be masked, when the person develops nonaffective symptoms (Worden, 1991).

There are normal manifestations of grief such as feelings of: sadness, anger, guilt and self-reproach, anxiety, loneliness, fatigue, helplessness, shock, emancipation, relief, and numbness. There is a thin line between grief and depression. It is true that grief looks very much like depression and it is also true that grieving may develop into full-blown depression

(Worden, 1991). Worden (1991) further stated that, "one of the functions of the counselor who has contact with people during time of acute grief is to assess which patients might be undergoing the development of a major depression." Grief can be an immediate or delayed experience that can be brief or it can go on for very long time. Each person's experience is different and consequently, each person will respond differently to grief.

BEREAVEMENT

According to the Living Webster Encyclopedic Dictionary of the English Language, bereavement comes from the word bereaved or bereft. It means to be deprived of someone loved or something that is prized. It is usually followed by bereavement which is the act of bereaving, deprivation, particularly the loss by death. People are dying every day and Christian people are not immune to death and dying. The death of a loved one deeply impacts the souls of individuals bereaved and can shake the foundations of one's family system (Clinton, 2005). Family relationships can fracture and splinter due the lack of proper bereavement counseling.

Death in a family can have deep spiritual implications and consequences for family members. A person's spirituality and religious beliefs may also have significant influences on the course of bereavement and especially the grief issue in which the bereaved is expected to accept the reality of death and adjust to an environment in which the deceased is missing (Clinton, 2005). While there are many different types of losses that can affect an individual's life and family, the loss that has a more lasting impact is that of bereavement. This type of loss sometimes impacts a local congregation and the pastor is expected to provide bereavement support. Hopefully, he has acquired the skillset to provide this caring service. The word of God is always comforting and scripture like Psalm 23; Joshua 1:9; Psalm 34:7,19; and Psalm 67:1-3, 7 are particularly helpful.

The deceased involvement in the activities of the local church may also demand that some level of bereavement support be provided for the entire congregation. Some pastors are ceasing the opportunity to form bereavement support group as they do divorce recovery groups. The support in bereavement should not be limited to the pastor, the entire church can be trained to get involved. The pastor however, should play the lead roll in this area and provide the needed guidance. Every church should have a bereavement support group with at least one trained personnel, volunteer or paid. It is the responsibility of the church to take care of the church.

Like mental health practitioners, every pastor should be educated in the area of bereavement counseling. The increase in school shooting in the United States in general is one of the reasons why pastors need to become more proficient in bereavement and grief counseling. Like adults, children and teens experience grief at the loss of a family member or friend. The lives of teens are already complex because of the many social and peer challenges they have to deal with on a daily basis. They must deal with hormone changes but life for the teen-in-grief is even more complex. The teens grief can also be compounded when a parent is not helpful (Perschy, 2004). This level of detachment is happening on a regular basis and most time it goes unnoticed and the can be scared for life.

The bereavement could be due to the death of a parent or a very close loved one. Perschy (2004) further states, that the surviving parent of a grieving teen may be so consumed by the pain of their own grief that there is little emotional energy left to deal with the grief of a son or daughter. This means that a sensitive and alert pastor would make sure that a parent group support is necessary to provide support for the parent. Perschy (2004) states also that, as the parent tend to their own grief, they will better be able to help their children, regardless of age. This need should never be underestimated because a grieving parent can get so consumed in their own grief that they neglect the children who are experiencing grief also. A sensitive clergyperson and a caring church can help such a family.

The pastoral counselor must be both spiritual and professional. There is such a thing as ministering through presence. Therapy and counseling is about processes and procedures. According to Neimeyer (2012), therapy begins with who we are, extends to what we do, and is manifested through our therapeutic presence that involves proper timing. It is important that the pastor be there with the mourner to engage in empathetic listening and provide pastoral presence. The therapist must embrace the emotional life of the grieving client and guide the client toward mindfulness (Neimeyer, 2012). How about guiding the client towards a knowledge of the creator, God? The scripture rightly used can bring about inner peace, comfort, and hope. Prayer can then be used as the intervention closure.

Many people are turning to mindfulness intervention as peace and comfort. A recent study has shown that mindfulness-based interventions (MBI) have been used effectively to treat depression, anxiety, and other mood disorders (Neimeyer,2012). This seems to open the flood gate for exploration with this technique. It is not beyond the pastor's calling or professional scope if he or she were to acquire the knowledge on mindfulness meditation. According to Epstein (1998), mindfulness meditation, like psychotherapy, hinges on showing us a new way to be with ourselves, and with others. Please understand, mindfulness meditation is more than a nice name and it is not recommended by me.

The Selah Grief Model, is a MBI that promise an enriching relationship between grieving clients and their clinicians. What is being emphasized here is a knowledge of mindfulness and not a practice of mindfulness. This knowledge is important because of creeping compromise into the Christian church. One could be indulging in Buddhism without knowing. Mindfulness meditation has its root in Buddhism and should not be practiced in Christianity. Meditation is a Christian teaching and practice. Mindfulness meditation is here mentioned only to alert Christian counselors about the subtlety in which this Buddhist teaching and practice can enter your congregation.

The Two-Track Model of Bereavement (TTMB) can help counselors and therapists coordinate therapeutic interventions in light of the client's needs, by drawing on it for conceptual, assessment and intervention purposes (Neimeyer, 2012). The Two-Track Model of Bereavement looks at the response to loss as requiring people to find a way to continue their lives, as well as to renegotiate the psychological relationship to the person who died (Neimeyer, 2012). Life must go on, but for that life to have any semblance of normalcy, the grieving client must be guided to map the rugged terrain of loss as he or she experiences the pain of grief. Grief is the unwanted price we pay for caring and loving and no one can escape its humbling effects. The scripture teaches that Jesus wept (John

11:35, Luke 19:41). Jesus experienced the pain of grief including all our other infirmities.

The recent spate of school violence in America has left a void and created the need for ongoing bereavement and grief counseling in affected schools. The children were traumatized by witnessing the violent deaths of their friends and school mates. According to Rynearson (1987), violent death is not only traumatizing but it includes the three Vs: violence, victimization, and violation. Those who are connected to the decease, can experience both separation distress or trauma distress. Flashbacks may begin to occur at a durable time and frequency. These flashbacks are customarily understood as posttraumatic stress disorder symptoms. Retelling the narrative can prove very helpful for the client (Neimeyer, 2012).

Every grieving person and mourner must get to the place where they can permit self to be healthy. If the mourner cannot permit self to be healthy, no treatment in the world will make a difference until that mourner decides it is permissible to let it go (Neimeyer, 2012). It is the responsibility of the therapist to listen acutely for any overt statement. Overt statements may be designed to be spoken directly to the relevant person.

The purpose of an overt statement is to induce an emotional deepening in any specific area selected by the therapist. Here highly personal phrases are used by the client in expressing key material that may have already emerge in less direct form (Neimeyer, 2012).

Life is made up of choices and even the grieving individual has to make a choice. Neimeyer (2012) asserts that it is important for the therapist to highlight that the client has a choice rather than directing the client to make a specific choice. The idea that the client can choose his or her attitude might be viewed as a cognitive reframing strategy (Neimeyer, 2012). Direct journaling can be used to facilitate meaning and disruptive life stories can become their effective self-narrative. This can be very effective especially for bereaved families with children and teenagers. The ability to move on after a significant loss calls for more than physical strength, emotional and spiritual strength are also needed. Many symbols can be employed to help in the grieving process.

Metaphors can be used as meaning-making symbols in treating trauma and grief while spirituality and religion continue to be indispensable to many who have a religious faith (Neimeyer, 2012). Art therapy plays its part especially with those who find it difficult to express themselves verbally and this can lead to opening up the photo album. Music therapy is also being used successfully in many ways, especially for those who have some level of music appreciation. Music therapy worked very well for King Saul and was the only therapy that worked as David played his harp. Is grief and mourning an endless hope? Will there always be something that will brings back the memories and the pain?

There is a sense in which mourning can be finished, when people regain an interest in life, feel more hopeful, experience gratification again, and adapt to new roles. There is also a sense in which mourning is never finished (Worden, 1991). Everyone at some point in their life experiences grief. Grief, like conflict can be considered an inescapable occurrence in life. It is important that pastors understand and even accept the reality that they are inadvertently faced with sickness and death daily. Therefore, they need to acquire some knowledge and techniques to provide bereavement and grief counseling to their parishioners.

A basic knowledge and understanding of grief will help pastors to apply creative practices in counseling the bereaved. With the exception of a patient in hospice care, most times the only person that a mourning and grieving family will ever meet to provide any form of spiritual support is the pastor. It is therefore, very important for the pastor to acquire some basic skills to complement his or her spiritual knowledge in ministering and counseling the bereaved. Gorer (1965) believes, that the way people respond to spoken condolences gives some indication of where they are in the mourning process. The local church pastor needs to have this basic knowledge in order to help the bereaving family back to wholeness. A visit and prayer always help but sometimes much more is needed and can be offered if the pastor has the skillset to provide bereavement counsel.

The grateful acceptance of condolences is one of the most reliable signs that the bereaved is working through mourning satisfactorily (Gorer, 1965). Hurt and pain are catalysis that help to draw people to seek God through a church family. Hurt and pain are often manifested through bereavement over the loss of a loved one. No single person can fully understand the depth of another person's grief. However, a pastoral counselor can and should know if the person is heading into depression and provide the necessary guidance for help.

CHAPTER 2

WHO ARE THE PEOPLE SITTING IN THE PEWS?

*T*he people who seem to need counseling every day are the disturbed and abused people, the perplexed and confused students, new comers to the community, the vocationally uncertain, convalescents, the aged, divorcees and potential divorcees, quarreling church members, the sick and terminally ill, the unemployed, and returned service personnel. This list represents some of the people who are sitting in the pews of churches each week. According to Clinton and Trent (2009), if you are a pastor or a church staff member, virtually everyone sitting in your pews today has been (or soon will be) touched by addiction, divorce, violence, depression, grief, confusion, loneliness, and a thousand other evidences of living as broken people in a fallen world, Clinton & Trent (2009). These broken people come week after week and participate in most of what goes on in church.

Worship may not solve their problems but gives them a sense of purpose and a keen sense of belonging. The afore mentioned groups form a very good cross section of the many people who will not confront the pastor with their problems, as real as they are. Any pastor who can become an expert in dealing with these problems, will have a very fruitful ministry (Kent, Sr. (1974). If solutions to these problems can be shared from the pulpit, more social, psychological, and spiritual healing would be seen in the church and the trauma of daily living greatly minimized. The reality is that most of these problems and issues are not being addressed from the twenty-first century pulpits of today.

TRAUMA FROM BIRTH TO DEATH

As the subject evolves, "The Relevance of Christian Counseling Today," How does this subject of trauma correlates with pastoral counseling ministry? The word, "Trauma" has multiple meanings that include but not limited to medical physical injury or psychological injury, as well as to the events that cause this injury. According to Terr (1991), traumatic events take many different forms such as "Type 1" which indicates a single-incident trauma and "Type 11" which indicates a complex or repetitive trauma. Terr (1991), supports the idea that physical and psychological trauma often co-occur but therapists follow the tradition of the field and focus on the psychological trauma. It is interesting to note, according to Weathers and Keane (2007), that psychological trauma does not have a clear definition, even in books on the topic.

Neurobiological and developmental research have revealed that psychological traumas are developmentally adverse if they block or interrupt the normal progression of psychological development in a child especially in infancy or early childhood. Such psychological development includes but not limited to: attention and learning, working, emotion regulation, personality formation, integration, and relationship. Parvizi and Damasio (2001), state that by age 2 years, the core self emerges with psychological capacities that are made possible by fully functional neural projections from the brainstem and midbrain. Assessment approaches to complex posttraumatic responses in children and adolescents are less developed than they are for adults. This is so because complex trauma has been less investigated in children and there are fewer measures available for assessing post-traumatic outcomes.

POST-TRAUMATIC STRESS DISORDER

The subjects of Post-Traumatic Stress Disorder and pastoral care should be topics for all pastors, pastoral counselors, chaplains, and all those in the caregiving field. The people sitting in the pews experience different forms of sufferings and traumas every day. Theodicy and suffering are not popular sermons in the pulpits of most pastors today. Some are afraid that sermonizing will bring back the sadness of their own sufferings and traumas. As a result, some congregations suffer because the pastor is ill-equipped to deal with such matters. Sometimes also, a pastor may not have gotten to the place of closure in his or her own experience of loss, and therefore, becomes numb or insensitive when he or she has to dealt with such, either from the pulpit or in the private setting of a parishioner's home.

Pastors nevertheless, must find ways to nurture themselves before they can effectively relate to their parishioners' transference, rejections, sufferings, and general trauma. Spirituality is a singular force of connection that the pastor must keep in the minds of his or her congregants. According to Rogers and Knoenig (2002), spirituality is the part of a person that searches for meaning, purpose, and relationship with others and with the transcendent, the divine, or the higher power. The pulpit should be used to educate and provide the hope that is needed after rape, post-traumatic stress disorder, and other forms of abuse.

Many twenty-first century pastors have limited the use of the twenty-first century pulpit to the preaching of a social gospel that appeals only to the emotions. Most of the social gospel that is preached emphasize individual prosperity over the core issues of divorce, trauma, anxiety, depression, delinquencies, and post-traumatic stress disorder to name a few. Going to heaven by living a Godfearing life is not the theme but living comfortably on earth is the goal to reach. The scripture warned us about this last day deception, stating that the time will come when men will not endure sound doctrine (2 Timothy 4: 3, 4). Consequently, social, marital, and physical trauma is generally missing from the pulpit because these subjects do not fit their prosperity model.

There are people attending church on a regular basis who are experiencing Post Traumatic Stress Disorder. My understanding is that PTSD generally develop from an outgrowth of the following: sexual trauma, physical trauma, psychological trauma, or spiritual trauma (Rogers & Knoenig, 2002). It is almost an impossibility to go through life without experiencing some form of trauma. Some casual factors include natural disasters, combat, hostage taking, prisoners of war, rape, ritual abuse, domestic violence, child abuse, elder abuse, and school or gang violence where life is threatened and are all psychological traumas (Rogers & Knoenig, 2002). It is interesting to note that all types of trauma impact spiritual trauma. Rogers & Knoenig (2002) further assert that spiritual trauma attacks the core of one's being and the meaning and purpose of one's life may become vague, confused, or lost.

One can understand therefore, why the clergy person needs to understand PTSD and how it impacts spirituality. It is amazing and gives reasons for great concern to realize the amount of people who are affected directly or indirectly with PTSD. It is an undisputable reality that our nation is greatly affected by PTSD due to the large-scale incidents of violence, natural disasters, and terrorist threats. The symptoms of PTSD can be seen all around us and they are not going away in a hurry. Interestingly, according to the DSM-1V-TR diagnostic criteria, a person who has exhibited the symptoms of PTSD for a month or longer qualifies for a PTSD diagnosis (Rogers & Knoenig, 2002). Everyone in the helping profession should be asking the question, what can I do to help?

PTSD symptoms fall into three categories namely: re-experiencing, avoidant/numbing, and hyperarousal. PTSD is not a difficult diagnosis to make if the clinician keeps the diagnostic criteria in mind. The clinician must acknowledge the patient's worse fears which helps to provide an environment of sensitivity, safety, and trust. The author revealed that most people who experience trauma do not develop PTSD, therefore it is all the more important for the clinician to understand who might be at greater risk. There are diagnostic and assessment tools available to the clinician for diagnosing PTSD. While the clergy person may not have the diagnostic tool, he or she should have a knowledge of what some of the signs are in order to make a timely referral.

These diagnostic instruments fall into three over-lapping categories: (1) Trauma Exposure Scale (2) Diagnostic Instruments and (3) Symptom Severity Scale. It is generally best to start with the Trauma Exposure Scale. According to Rogers & Knoenig (2002), sometimes comorbid disorder must be treated before PTSD treatment can begin, and sometimes therapy is combined with medication. This is one of the reasons why the pastoral counselor must have the basic knowledge so that the proper referral can be made. This level of treatment would be beyond the skillset of the pastoral counselor but not beyond his knowledge scope.

EARLY LIFE TRAUMA

It is clear that early life trauma can affect normal developmental processes and if corrective measures are not taken early they will reflect in the adult life. Courtois and Ford (2009) reveal and share some of the best practices in psychotherapy for children, adolescents, and adults experiencing complex traumas and stress disorders. The use of Contextual Behavior Trauma Therapy (CBTT) by therapists in developing a sense of self was quite revealing. CBTT integrates techniques from Acceptance Behavior Therapy (ACT), Dialectical Behavioral Therapy (DBT), and Functional Analytic Psychotherapy (FAP) in working with clients with complex traumatic stress disorders (Courtois & Ford, 2009). This is encouraging and hopeful for the client because complex trauma may need different types of treatment plans and therapeutic interventions to ascertain the best fit.

Courtois & Ford (2002) were very clear to point out that, regardless of the specific diagnosis or assessment and treatment methodologies in use, the core problems of affect dysregulation, structural dissociation, somatic dysregulation, impaired self-development, and disorganized attachment patterns are likely to remain the foundation for clinicians working with survivors of complex trauma. Again, I emphasize the reason for timely and appropriate referrals when the need arises. Life is precious and an early detection can facilitate early treatment to keep a potentially deadly disease in check. There is a tremendous need for Christian counselors today who can look with diagnostic eyes for the onset of different diseases.

A trained therapist can integrate Accelerated Experiential Dynamic Psychotherapy (AEDP) and Emotion-Focused Therapy for Trauma (EFTT) into a treatment plan (Courtois & Ford, 2002). A pastoral counselor would know that this would be beyond his scope and expertise. A therapist would have the ability and therapeutic sensitivity to know when to introduce Emphatic Exploration (EE) and Imaginal Confrontation (IC) as interventions, a pastoral counselor is therapeutically limited. The goal of EE or IC initially is to help the client to shift from expressions of undifferentiated hurt and global distress to more differentiated expressions of adaptive anger and sadness (Courtois & Ford, 2009).

It appears that every therapeutic intervention can be used at some point in time to help a client with post-traumatic stress disorder. From Cognitive Behavioral Therapy to Cognitive-Behavioral Intervention for Traumatized Students (CBITS). The key to effective and corrective treatment is proper assessment. Assessment is so important that psychometric assessment of complex clinical cases has come to rely on sophisticated interviews and procedures, and a variety of measures that extend beyond the symptoms of specific psychiatric disorders (Courtois & Ford, 2009). In any given situation, proper assessment will lead to correct diagnosis that will ultimately result in the right intervention and treatment.

THEODICY AND HUMAN SUFFERING

Theodicy and human suffering are not easily understood by the ordinary lay person and yet they may be the most to be affect. Since Adam's time every human being has been involved in the consequences of the first sin. Each child has been born into a sinful human family and each has inherited the weaknesses and perverted tendencies resulting from sin (Jemison, 1959). At the beginning man walked and talked with God in the Garden in the cool of the day and it is logical to conclude that God counseled with man at such time (Gen. 3:8). Jay Adams asserts that the pre-fall fellowship was unbroken and entirely open, and the counsel consisted of positive, good, beneficial revelation calculated to develop man's full potential (Adams, 1979).

The door to human suffering and trauma was opened when man first doubted God by believing Satan's lie, Gen. 3:3-5. This counsel not to eat of the fruit of the tree was necessary for man's well-being. He was dependent upon it and was held responsible for obeying it (Adams, 1979). The question that Satan asked was an attack on God's good counsel. Man's sad plight began not so much from the time he sinned but from the time he entertained doubt. That doubt meant that, if not then, later he would still sin. Doubt and mistrust are the results of this original sin and ultimate sickness and death. The Plan of Salvation is the only escape route from this sinful dilemma. God has provided a way of excape from every sin and temptation man may encounter (1 Cor. 10:13).

Sin by nature, is a traumatic experience. It is not unusual therefore, for victims of trauma to feel that God is punishing them for something they have done or not done (Rogers, 2002). The spiritual care provider must understand that in a unique way, he or she is representing Christ to the traumatized and suffering person. The spiritual care provider must be willing to listen with empathy and compassion and hear even what is not said in order to initiate healing. This calls for much tact and patience on the part of the spiritual care provider.

Theodicy and human suffering are not easily understood by the ordinary lay person and yet they may be affected the most. It is not unusual for victims of trauma to feel that God is punishing them for something they have done or not done. Therefore, the spiritual care provider must be willing to listen with empathy and compassion and hear even what is not said in order to initiate healing. Meaning is found within oneself therefore, everyone needs to tell his or her story. Sharing one's story calls for a measure of trust because your story is an expression of the inner you and your journey be it good or bad. The person who tells his or her story must be willing to become vulnerable and an expression of anger can also be a manifestation of storytelling. As the story is told the pastoral counselor or spiritual care provider must be prepared to hear anything and everything without appearing to be shocked or become judgmental

It is important to encourage appropriate expression of anger and to assist the survivor in this endeavor (Rogers & Knoenig, (2002). Sometimes pastors may find that they are the object of displaced anger. This should be ok as long as the pastors refuse to take any-thing personal. Some people even get angry at God when thing go contrary to their expectation and belief. When anger is openly expressed it can help to lay the foundation to introduce prayer, meditation, and other healing practices. At this time the ministry of presence is very effective. The pastoral counselor would do well to just sit and listen to the survivor as he or she vents. This is therapeutic for the survivor and very necessary for moving forward.

DOMESTIC VIOLENCE

Domestic violence is another area of human reality that is seldom addressed from the pulpit. Domestic vio-lence is on the increase even in the church. This is evidence of a deep spiritual problem. A pastor should be able to help someone to reclaim their spirituality as a source of healing and empowerment and thereby develop a renewed sense of hope and a more realistic and balanced view of the world (Rogers & Knoenig, 2002). The moral fabric of our nation is eroding at a rapid pace and the spiritual foundation is shaking meaning that it is no longer firm. When the home and family is under moral and spiritual siege by the devil, the end results are what is seen in the manifestations of the different forms of domestic violence. If the foundation of the home is weak, then the community will be weak, and ultimately the nation.

The pulpit is a good place to initiate corrective measures and provide generalized help for the abused and the abuser. This is very important because the abused person will sometime tolerate the abuse for years before coming forward. Sometimes silence becomes golden because the abuser holds a leading and influential position in the church. The abused person may even be the pastor's wife, worse yet, the pastor himself. In such cases, the subject would definitely be kept out of the pulpit. The price of silence affects the children in an abusive family. Children who grow up exposed to an abusive father's behavior learn that abuse is the price people pay if they want to receive love (Bancroft, 2002).

Children are the ones affected the most when spouses abuse each other. They grow up with a deep sense of insecurity and fear. Their worse fear is that one day their mother and father will separate and this is a devastating experience. Some children may even begin to act out their fears and insecurities at school and other places. Younger children may even begin to wet their bed and start failing in school. These are some of the issues that need to be addressed from the pulpit and thereby creating a sense of awareness and education. While the abused may feel a sense of pride and is forced to keep silent, the child or children can be encouraged to speak out in order to get help for themselves and possibly the abused.

WHAT IS DOMESTIC VIOLENCE?

What really constitute domestic violence? This question is still being researched by social scientists to arrive at a more definitive answer. However, Potter-Efron (2015) provides an open window to a definition and understanding. He states, that domestic violence is battering, spouse abuse, intimate partner violence, intimate partner abuse, and domestic violence. All these terms have been used to describe physical and verbal behaviors that hurt, intimidate, or diminish a close family member (usually but not always a relationship partner) (Potter-Efron, 2015). Domestic violence is also known as domestic abuse. It includes family violence, dating violence, courting violence, and intimate partner violence.

Domestic violence is really a pattern of behavior that involves abuse by one partner against another in an intimate relationship. Domestic violence may refer to a single event or to a continuing pattern of behavior. It may refer to impulsive, unplanned behaviors, or to carefully constructed plans carried out over months or years (Potter-Efron, 2015). Domestic violence is not confined to only the poor. It is not socially, culturally, educationally, or spiritually confined. Domestic violence is perpetrated in every nook and cranny of our nation. It is evidence that Satan has a grip on many lives and this is one of his means to destroy Christian homes and families through warped and misguided love. Domestic violence is social, mental, and spiritual problem that is pandemic in nature.

Sometimes the pulpits of some churches are used unconsciously to plant the seed for domestic violence. This unconscious misuse of some pulpits is seen in the use of scriptures that are twisted to justify domestic violence. Victims who are Christians often stay in abusive relationships because Scriptures misquoted and misrepresented from the pulpit do not seem to give them any other option (Dunbar, 2016). The New Testament is replete with such scriptures some of which include: Matthew 5:38,39; Ephesians 5:23, 24; 1Peter 3:1; 1Cor.7:4; and Matthew 5:24 to name a few. It is evil to the highest order for any pastor, the shepherd of the flock, to use the scripture and misrepresent the word of God to give credence to abuse.

An abuser can be a skillful manipulator and he knows exactly what hurts the most. Children are a tempting weapon for an abuser to use against the mother. Nothing inflicts more pain on a caring parent, male or female, than hurting one of his or her children or causing damage to the parent-child relationship (Bancroft, 2002). Life with an abuser in the home can both stressful and scary. They listen to the arguments filled with threats; they feel the tension; they see the tears of mother and sometimes feel it is their fault. Some abuser will go as far as to threatens to kill the child if the mother does not do what he requires. It is difficult for one who is not in the situation to fully understand why a mother would not scream for help.

A pastor has a special role to play as the spiritual leader of his or her congregation. A pastor must be equipped to provide support and even care to a parishioner who is experiencing domestic violence. Rightly dividing the word of truth is one of the roles of the pastor and spiritual leader. There are scriptures to reinforce and support an abuse free relationship. Such scriptures include: "so husbands must love their own wives as their own bodies; he who loves his wife loves himself. For no one ever hates his own flesh, but nourishes and cherishes it, just as the Lord does the church" (Ephesians 5:28,29); "husbands, in the same way be considerate as you live with your wives and treat them with respect as the weaker partner and as heirs with you of the gracious gift of life, so that nothing will hinder your prayers" (1 Peter 3:7).

Apart from physical abuse that manifest itself outwardly, domestic abuse can easily be concealed by the offended. The local church should and can assume responsibility for restoring distressed people suffering from personal ineffectiveness to full, productive, joyful lives. In order to do this the local church must develop its unique resources for counseling, Crabb (1977). Christian counselors must turn to scripture that can be used to liberate victim of domestic violence that might be sitting in the pews each week. "For God has not given us a spirit of fear, but of love, power, and a sound mind" (2 Timothy 1:7). Abusers need liberation also and they must not be left on the sidelines, they are also sitting in the pews.

THE ROLE OF ANGER IN
DOMESTIC VIOLENCE

Anger is a common human emotion that can be triggered by fear, threat, jealousy, insecurity, abandonment, loss, loss of control, intoxication, and hatred. While anger does not cause violence, it is an emotion many men exploit when things are not going as they want. Men who batter typically use anger as a way to control their partners and show displeasure (Paymar, 2000). Anger may be the singular emotion that is used to conceal real fear by parading demagoguery. The angry person wants to be seen and heard therefore, is always loud and verbose while deep inside maybe scared and afraid.

The society and culture in which we live creates a fertile ground for birthing anger among men. The expectations of society and the perceptions of what make a man, a man all add to their confusion. The bar had been set by the Superman myth, John Wayne the quintessential tough-guy, Clint Eastwood, Chuck Norris, and more recently Luke Cage, George Clooney, Brad Pitt, Tom Cruise, and Denzil Washington. According to Paymar (2000), if being a man means strength and toughness, then what are you if you fail to meet these expectations of being a man? You are a failure, a sissy, or a coward. It is possible that some of the battered women, some of the abused wives may have used this type of condescending language and comparative overtures to their men that triggers their anger?

There is a theory called the "Anger Cause Violence" Theory. In the Anger Cause Violence Theory, the practitioner views the client as having poor impulse control or having adopted patterns of reaching to conflict or stress with aggression. The inherent assumption is that the offender's stress and anger build until an incident triggers a violent outburst (Paymar, 2000). Practitioners believe that anger management can be taught and used in such a way that the offender will not batter by focusing on physical and emotional cues when upset or angry. Although the scripture speaks against anger and does show where it has its place, many Christians do get overwhelmed by anger (Eph. 4:26).

It is very important for the pastors or pastoral counselors to know how to detect and manage anger. The physical signs of anger might be tightened fists, clenched teeth, or rapid breathing. Emotional signs might be stress, anxiety, or feeling hurt or put down. Offenders are taught deescalating techniques, time-out techniques, meditation, deep-breathing, and self-talk (Paymar, 2000). These techniques work best as pre- ventions measures. The most effective strategy and technique is the time-out technique, when the offender removes himself from a conflict if he feels he is on the verge of becoming abusive.

Anger is not just about one's emotion, it is also about choice. Exhaustive research has shown that cli- ents can change from being chronically angry and destructive to becoming emotionally balanced (Paymar, 2000). This should not be surprising because nothing is impossible with God. Therapeutically, angry and aggressive behavior may be best altered through pro- grams that provide and promote attachment to others and help the client to address their initial protective and defensives reactions to perceive threat (Paymer, 2000). Rage is anger in action and there are five dif- ferent types of rage. Rage according to Paymer (2000) is an experience of tremendous fury, far more intense than strong anger. It is therefore, incumbent on the counselor to help the client to identify which of the five rages pattern identifies their behavior.

Anger can be very resistant to corrective treatment. Therefore, proper assessment is of vital importance. A pastoral counselor's ability to make this initial assessment is invaluable because he or she would be better able to make a timely referral. Paymer (2000), highlighted two standardized assessment that are particularly useful. They are the State-Trait Anger Expression Inventory—11 and the Anger Disorder Scale. The first is an easy to use questionnaire that taps several important areas of anger and good in developing treatment plan. Pastoral counselors should get acquainted with the questionnaire format of assessment to use in their everyday counseling ministry.

The Anger Disorder Scale uses a structured interview format called the Structured Interview for Anger Disorders which are based on five domains. These five domains are provocations, cognitions, motives, arousal, and behavior. This clinical assessment tool is more appropriate for the professional therapist. According to Paymer (2000), a thorough assessment is the first step toward successful anger management counseling. Although assessment and treatment are often treated as separate entities, the reality is that treatment begins with assessment and that assessment continues throughout treatment.

Most act and outburst of domestic violence can be considered an outgrowth of anger. It can be described as physical and verbal behavior that hurt, intimidate, or diminish a close family member including a relationship partner. Domestic violence can be a single event or a continuing pattern of behavior. Anger and domestic abuse are triggers for traumatic stress disorder. People with Post Traumatic Stress Disorder (PTSD) need to know that the pastoral counselor cares and is in a trusting and unique position to display support and compassionate care.

Sometimes the ministry of presence is needed more than counsel. Trauma is not just an external catastrophic event that happened to an individual who was in the wrong place at the wrong time. According to Potter-Efron (2015), the concept of trauma has changed from being considered a rare external event (DSM-111) to an individual's psychological response to a not-uncommon, overwhelming event (DSM-1V).

Although an abuser prefers to have you wholeheartedly on his side, he will settle contentedly for your decision to take a middle stance, because, to him, that means you see the couple's problems as partly her fault and partly his fault, which means it is not abuse (Bancroft, 2002). Everyone should read Dr. Judith Herman master piece on "Trauma and Recovery" in which "neutrality" actually serves the interests of the perpetrator much more that those of the victim and so is not neutral (Bancroft, 2002).

Only people who respond to catastrophic events with fear, helplessness, or horror have been "traumatized" as defined in DSM-1V(TR). A person must therefore, experience trauma-related symptoms and impairments in everyday functioning for at least a month before diagnostic assessment for PTSD would be appropriate (Potter-Efron, 2015). It is not recommended that the pastoral counselor venture beyond this point unless he or she has specialized training in this area of expertise. It is therefore, time for this parishioner or client to be referred to a more competent professional.

The pastoral caregiver must always be aware of gender issues and sexuality and have a keen sense of human sensitive and emotion. Race, class, and multi-culturalism can also impact the pastoral caregiver and it is also important to understand that social stigma is attached to certain death, like suicide (Rogers & Knoenig, 2002). Most people are not expecting the pastor to have all the answers, but he or she should possess common knowledge on how to make referrals to other professionals and to whom specific referrals should be made in the event of certain crisis.

The pastoral counselor should also be familiar with his or her denominational guidelines as it relates to duration of counseling time on a particular issue. It is highly recommended that all active clergy members have a supervisor, mentor, or professional counselor that they see on a regular basis to debrief their reactions, projections, transference, or countertransference, or other concerns as they provide pastoral care (Rogers & Knoenig, 2002). No pastor should ever feel alone and without support. A pastor should be a professional and of such should have access to some form of peer interaction and review.

Domestic violence can be considered an outgrowth of anger. It can be described as physical and verbal behavior that hurt, intimidate, or diminish a close family member including a relationship partner. Domestic violence can be a single event or a continuing pattern of behavior. Potter-Efron (2015) reveal that there is a cycle to anger and aggression that impacts domestic violence. The following are the six phases in this cycle or model to anger and aggression: activation, modulation, preparation, action, feedback, and deactivation. Potter-Efron further states that, "the activation stage is where therapist face their greatest challenge in the anger cycle." Chronically angry families can be a danger to themselves and society. These family members seldom take responsibility for their own actions and everybody blames each other (Potter-Efron, 2015).

As a Christian woman and a wife, I did not fully grasp the reality that a wife could actually be raped by her own husband because the Bible teaches that the spouse should render his or her conjugal rights (1Cor.7:3-4). It is now a generally accepted philosophy and a law in some states, that any forced sexual activity either by threat, intimidation, physical overpowering, or any unwanted means, may be considered rape, even if it involves a spouse. This reality has gotten the vote of seventeen states including the District of

Columbia in which no exemption from rape prosecution is granted to husbands.

It is the general belief that more wives will come forward and when this happens, all the remaining states will sign on. The trend has already begun recently with the cadre of women who have come forward with their sexual harassment claims in high places. Many lives have been traumatized because of violence that is perpetrated mainly against women. Many women are still keeping silent because of the shame, while many others feel it is their duty to protect the perpetrators. Education is urgently needed and the pulpit is one of the places that can be effectively used as an education source.

It is generally understood that PTSD develops from an outgrowth of one of the followings: sexual trauma, physical trauma, psychological trauma, or spiritual trauma. According to Rogers & Knoenig (2002), natural disasters, combat, hostage taking, prisoners of war, rape, ritual abuse, domestic violence, child abuse, elder abuse, and school or gang violence where life is threatened are all psychological traumas. It is interesting to note that all types of trauma impact spiritual trauma. Rogers & Knoenig (2002) further assert, that spiritual trauma attacks the core of one's being and the meaning and purpose life may become vague, confused, or lost.

One can understand therefore, why the clergy person needs to understand PTSD and how it impacts spirituality. It is amazing and gives reasons for great concern to realize the amount of people who are affected directly or indirectly with PTSD. Our nation is greatly affected by PTSD due to the large-scale incidents of violence, natural disasters, and terrorist threats. The symptoms of PTSD can be seen all around us. Interestingly, according to the DSM-1V-TR diagnostic criteria, a person who has exhibited the symptoms of PTSD for a month or longer qualifies for a PTSD diagnosis.

THE PASTOR AS CAREGIVER
AND COUNSELOR

A pastor has a special role to play as the spiritual leader of his or her congregation. A pastor must be equipped to provide support and even care to a parishioner with PTSD. A pastor should be able to help someone to reclaim their spirituality as a source of healing and empowerment and thereby develop a renewed sense of hope and a more realistic and balanced worldview (Rogers & Knoenig, 2002). People with PTSD need to know that you care and the pastor is in a trusting and unique position to display support and compassionate care. Sometimes the ministry of presence is needed more than counsel.

The pastoral counselor should also be familiar with his or her denominational guidelines as it relates to duration of counseling time on a particular issue. It is highly recommended that all active clergy members have a supervisor, mentor, or professional counselor that they see on a regular basis. This professional encounter provides the opportunity to debrief their reactions, projections, transference, or countertransference, or other concerns as they provide pastoral care (Rogers & Knoenig, 2002). The pastoral caregiver must always be aware of gender issues and sexuality and have a keen sense of human sensitivity and emotion.

According to Rogers; race, class, and multiculturalism can also impact the pastoral caregiver. It is also important to understand that social stigma is attached to certain death, like suicide (Rogers & Knoenig, 2002). People are not expecting the pastor to have all the answers, but he or she should possess common knowledge on how to make referrals to other professionals and to whom specific referrals should be made in the event of certain crisis. The preaching pulpit must be used for more than preaching the gospel. It must also be used to provide a framework for physical, mental, and social healing.

SUICIDE AND SUICIDE IDEATION

Suicide has gotten so prevalent among all age groups in America that it is fast becoming a normative act. Pastors and pastoral counselors can no longer sit back and watch the further escalation of this problem without attempting to do something to reverse the trend. There are people sitting in the pews who are entertaining suicide ideation. A little knowledge, a little training, and a little clinical perception to know what to look for and listen to, can save many lives. Some who are committing suicide are taking many other lives with them in the process.

Like most people, the subject of suicide in general is not one of my subjects of choice. The reality and causes of suicide being a fact of life have become an eye-opening experience. Every parent should want to know more about suicide and suicide prevention because it could be lurking right at their doors. Any training in family counseling that does not include the understanding and prevention of suicide is incomplete. It would be well for all clergy persons to take a course in suicide prevention. Social and academic pressures are two prominent causal factors.

The causes for suicide among adolescents are many and varied and there are many more questions than answers. The statistics on adolescent suicide rate between 1960 and 1988 is stunning. The general population for the same period increased by approximately 17 % while the adolescent suicide rate rose by 200% (Capuzzi, 2009). It is time for suicide prevention be taught in our school and high time for it to become a subject from the preacher's pulpit. David Capuzzi provides middle and high school counselors with assistance and guidelines in the process of dealing with youth suicide problem in our schools (Capuzzi, 2009). The different entities and institutions involve in prevention is very encouraging but their effectiveness is yet to be seen.

As a person of faith, I take God at his word when he said that it is not his will for any to perish. Suicide is not in his plan for mankind therefore, there is always a way out. Knowing the family history and understanding the triggers are very important. Bertini (1955) states, that a child is shaped and influenced from the womb. If the home environment is toxic to good communication and healthy lifestyle, a place where alcohol is abused and parental fighting is habitual, then "the seeds for environmental depression could compound the genetic susceptibility obtained from the birth mother." Drinking alcohol, smoking cigarettes, and using substances can also affect the fetus (Bertini, 1955). Bertini (1955) further asserts, that the ground work for genetically transmitting physical imperfections such as multiple sclerosis, cancer, and Alzheimer's is laid in the first months of life.

It is undisputable then, that children with mental health issues such as anxiety, depression, attention deficit disorder, bipolar disorder, and autism are high risk for suicide. These children will further be at a disadvantage if they do not have at least one parent who understands the nature of their illness (Bertini, 1955). Worse yet, if their teacher is impatient and unskilled in the area of detecting mal-adaptive behavioral pattern, their problem is compounded even in the classroom.

This lack in teacher skill is see quite often in the area of a student with Attention Deficit Disorder. Bertini (1955) further asserts, that psychopathology is probably the single most frequently studied factor in the research literature on suicidal behaviors.

The large majority of suicidal youth are afflicted with one or another form of psychopathology (Wagner, 2009). Researchers have provided suggestive evidence that individuals who were abused or experienced other maladaptive parenting during childhood may find it extremely difficult to make and maintain friendships as adolescents, which in turn places them at risk for suicidal behavior (Johnson et al., 2002). This information can help to save lives and regulate extreme behaviors if it is presented in a didactic type of sermon from the pulpits of churches.

SUICIDE PREVENTION

David Miller is an accomplished school psychologist who left no stone unturned in laying out how child and adolescent suicide occurs from ideation to suicide-related communications, to suicide attempts, and suicide (Miller, 2011). Presently, there is a school-base suicide prevention program that is curriculum-based, classroom centered, and lecture-discussion oriented (Miller, 2011). This school-based suicide prevention program however, is only provided at the high school level. Due to the seriousness of suicide and the urgent need to control it or remove it from our schools, it should be in the curriculum for our middle schools also.

Law makers, educators, psychologists and counselors need to come together and create an aggressive but simple suicide prevention education program that targets elementary school children. Children grow up and become parents therefore, it is best to begin to teach children about suicide prevention, so that when they become parents they can spot early suicidal pattern and behavior in their children. Suicide is already affecting their young lives directly and indirectly. We are not protecting them when we don't teach them, we are exposing them and making them vulnerable.

There is no reason for a middle-schooler to commit suicide. Nevertheless, this is happening in our schools at an alarming rate. It is obvious that the problem of suicide in our schools is not going away and it is not being controlled. Therefore, the institution that is responsible to educate our children for life and living should be more intentional and direct in crafting a curriculum that meets a growing need. Like a tornado on its path of destruction, the violence has made a turn and is now invading our churches. This turn may awaken the need for pastoral involvement in a more intentional manner.

Miller (2011), alluded to the success seen in the suicide prevention program in Miami-Dade School District. This is success that can be improved upon and expanded to reach the entire United States. Regardless of the measured success in that particular program, if early childhood education were to include suicide prevention, even in the form of cartoon characterization, the schools and society would begin to see a positive change. Schools are about education and real education is about life and living. Therefore, it is time for this societal ill, be given the attention it deserves. Attention means serious, purposeful, and intentional governmental investment in research and program implementation to educate parents and children concerning the importance of life and the evil of suicide.

It is in fact very difficult for schools to build in the curriculum the reality and equality of life, because some teachers in the system were raised with a prejudicial mindset and this is inadvertently displayed in the classroom. The American Constitution states that all men are created equal and are entitled life, liberty, and the pursuit of happiness. The government is instituted to protect these rights. The problem is, it is hard to exercise a right when that right is not made a subject to be taught with pride and passion. The question that all who are concerned must ask is this; is it possible that a major part of the problem is embedded in the American value system?

A value system that educates just the head but not the heart will ultimately fail. A value system that is slowly taking away parental rights in lieu of the children rights will also fail. A value system where parents have to get their child's permission to access their grades from school is already a failure. The problem of child and adolescent suicide is deeper than what meets the eye. It is embedded deep within our value system and is a missing link in our school curriculum. The values that must be taught and can lift this nation out of this quagmire, unfortunately, will be met with opposition even from among many misguided parents. These are some of the things that are missing from the twenty-first century pulpit, while the members are suffering in the pews.

Many schools have become more aggressive in preparing their staff concerning policies and guidelines concerning suicide ideation and communication because of the litigious nature of our society. School personnel have been sued for actions such as failing to notify parents regarding their child's suicidal communication (Miller, 2011). The litigious stance many of the schools have taken, now forces them to embrace Best Practices. Best Practices is informed by legal requirements and ethical responsibilities, but need not be limited to them (Miller, 2011). School administrators appear to be more concerned with protection against lawsuits than fighting the problem of suicide in the schools.

Suicide is not just a Public Health tragedy, it is a national tragedy. Public health is what we, as a society, do collectively to assure the conditions in which people can be healthy (Miller, 2011). There needs to be a more aggressive plan also for public education about suicide prevention. The prevention programs of the public health model are very good. The universal suicide prevention program is also very good, but these programs should be used to complement an early childhood education program. Children should be taught that it is always right to break a promise of secrecy if by breaking that promise, it will save a life. This is very important because a child will share with a peer quicker than with an adult.

The term called "safety contracting" sometimes called, "no suicide" contract is one that needs to be understood. The issue of safety contracting arises in almost any discussion of management of acute suicide risk (Wagner, 2009). A safety contract typically involves an agreement between the client and the clinician that the client will not attempt suicide and will notify someone (a parent, the therapist, another trusted adult, a suicide hotline) if a suicidal urge arises (Wagner, 2009). There is no evidence to show that safety contract actually works in preventing suicide (Jobes, 2003).

Statistics have shown that there are an estimated 50,000 suicides in America each year and about 200,000 survivor victims (Capuzzi, 2009). These numbers are alarming but if the nation does not become intentional in its education programs as it relates to prevention, these numbers may have already increased. It is high time therefore, for lawmakers at every level of government here in the United States to recognize that the present program for suicide prevention in the schools is inadequate. Every teacher from every level of middle school and high school should be taught or made knowledgeable in detecting suicidal tendencies. School administrations must be purposeful and intentional about this because the problem is not going away anytime soon.

SUBSTANCE ABUSE AND ADDICTION

Substance abuse and addiction have become a pervasive problem in the United States and a solution to this growing problem is remote. Substance abuse and addiction is in every village and every hamlet, in every nook and crannies of our developed nation. It seems to be out of control at every level and the sad part is that it appears as if someone or an organization is benefiting from it. Therapists and counselors, including pastoral counselors need to document addiction as one of the problems that ranks among the top health and social issues in the United States. In 2017 the surgeon general declared that America has an opioid crisis.

The statistics on the age range of abusers and addicts, the many different types of drugs, the annual cost, and the high death rate are all alarming. Weaver et al. (2007)

state, that drugs and alcohol cost Americans more than $294 billion annually in preventable expenses and lost productivity. Problem gambling is another addiction that is showing a sharp increase. In my opinion, more is being done to sustain the problem than to control or eliminate it. Casinos are still being built and more licenses are being issued to open liquor stores and bars. The reality is that the government and lawmakers are a part of the problem, because they have made it too easy to obtain and maintain liquor license. Our country has become a country of addicts.

It has become an urgent need for clergy persons to be informed as to how to recognize addiction. Research over several decades has demonstrated that millions of Americans call upon clergy for help in times of trouble, which includes dealing with problems related to addiction (Weaver et al., 2007). Weaver et al. (2007) further assert that, "Clergy in the African American Communities considers drug abuse as the number one problem in their communities." It is clear that faith communities can offer supportive environments that can reinforce family attitudes and teachings against substance abuse.

Alcohol addiction is only one of the forms of addiction, yet only a very small minority of churches get involved to do anything to help. Alcoholic Anonymous is the general program that few faith-based organizations embrace and support. Addiction is a real problem and pastors need to be intentional in addressing this problem from their pulpits. Even if the members are not directly involved, they have family members who are addicts and need help. A little education can go a long way.

Weaver et al. (2007), shared different case studies and outlined the steps a caring pastor would take in trying to counsel a parishioner who needs help with addiction. The book, "Counseling Persons with Addiction and Compulsion: A Handbook for Clergy and other Helping Professionals" is one that every twenty-first century clergy person should read. In this book is found the diagnostic criteria, the use of the Diagnostic and Statistical Manual (DSM), and the responses to the different vignettes to be particularly interesting and insightful. The ability to diagnosed and recognize addiction or other forms of abuse can help the clergy person and counselor to know when to refer the parishioner for specialized professional help because of his or her own limitations.

Chapter 3

The Need for Christian Counseling

*J*n the Christian religion the Bible is generally accepted as the authoritative, infallible revelation of God's character and will. Adams states that the bible is the basis for Christian counseling and Christian counseling is about changing lives by changing values, beliefs, attitudes, relationships, and behaviors (Adams, 1979). Life in general is all about relationship. The vertical relationship between man and God and the horizontal relationship between man and his fellowmen.

If Christian counseling is to be effective, the counselor must have more than a parochial knowledge of the bible. According to Adams (1979), the counselor's ability to use the scripture in counseling should never be called into question. The counselor must be converted and is able to demonstrate that there is biblical authority for the directions he or she gives a counselee. Every counselee should know that they are in the presence of a Christian counselor therefore, they should expect the scripture to be used.

Christian counseling should not be limited to the clergy person. Christians should embrace the concept of the priesthood of all believers. This means that every Christian is called to a ministry of helping and encouraging other, especially those in the household of faith (Crabb, 1977). The major task is to discover the spiritual gifts of a congregation and encourage as many as possible to be specifically trained for a specialized ministry of counseling involving a deeper exploration into stubborn problems. Every church should have trained and committed members on the pastoral staff who can help with the counseling needs in the church.

The bible teaches that we are our brother's keeper therefore, no effort must be spared in trying to help anyone in need. Crabb (1977) asserts, the goal of biblical counseling is to promote Christian maturity, to help people enter into a richer experience of worship and a more effective life of service. Man will continue to run away from the one he needs most, God.

Interestingly however, from the very day man sinned, God went in search of man (Gen. 3:8,9).

Christians who understand the nature of God, understand Him to be omnipotent, omnipresence, omniscience, and immutable. Man cannot escape God, neither can he escape God's love and mercy. People need a fresh concept of the nature of God. A counselee can no more avoid and ignore God than he can live without air, God is his atmosphere (Adams, 1979). The bible teaches that while we were yet sinners, Christ died for us (Rom. 5:8). This means that while we were living in defeat, without any hope, God sent His Son to die for us. We must now trust Him to save us because we certainly cannot save ourselves from the condemnation of sin.

God wants us to be in constant communication with him and prayer is that vehicle that is made available to us to communicate with God. It makes much sense therefore, for counselees and all Christians to learn to pray. God however, does not limit himself to communicate to us only through prayer. God uses several other intermediaries to communicate to us. The Written Word, the Living Word, and Nature are but a few of the way in which God communicates with man. The Holy Spirit, the third person of the Godhead, plays an important role and must be understood. Jesus the Christ lived among men and he was the greatest psychologist who ever walked this earth. Nevertheless, there is an ongoing problem of integrating Christianity with psychology.

Bible students know and understand that Christ taught in parables not so much to protect himself from those who wanted to shut him up, but more so to provide a frame of reference for the common people to understand the message. Psychology has its place in ministry although secular psychologists may think otherwise. Crabb (1977) states, psychology and its specialized discipline of psychotherapy offer some valid insights about human behavior which in no way contradict scripture. Christianity is not empirical in its scope because Christianity is not about works that you can measure, but rather about faith that works. Psychology according to my understanding is all about empiricism, Christianity is more subjective and should be subjected to subjective interpretation.

Christian counselors should continue to press cautiously towards the integration of Christianity and psychology. However, as they move forward, special care must be taken to protect and safe guard our biblical foundation and principles. It is quite clear that humanistic philosophy and teachings have pose a problem for Christian counselors because humanism puts human being in the place of God. General counselors seek to help human beings to change by focusing on human beings themselves.

The main problem is that, without God no genuine or lasting change can take place. When Adam and Eve sinned, they had fallen so far that the image of God in them was almost obliterated and needed to be renewed (James 3:9; Eph. 4:23). Like Adam, we are gregarious beings, we like company and have a yearning desire for fellowship. The devil capitalizes on this innate nature to socialize and uses it against man especially in broken marriages. There is a need for Christian counseling today.

There is a need for Christian counselors who can help Christians find God's solutions to their human problems caused by sin. Sin is the foundation of guilt and misery and it affects our very thinking (Crabb, 1977). Therefore, Christian counselors must teach their counselees to rethink the problem. Most counselees think improperly and therefore their perception and concept of God and who God is also is incorrect. Consequently, forgiveness must become an important subject in Christian counseling, because the counselee must learn to accept God's forgiveness and also forgive himself or herself.

I have seen Christian couples in conflict who fail to forgive each other. The result is bitterness, resentment, hatred, and ultimate divorce. Christians are forgiven people who should be thankful for it and should be willing to give it as much as receive it. Repentance and confession are inextricably bound to confession. I believe however, that forgiveness does more for the offended than the offender. The true Christian will always seek to forgive because forgiveness is one evidences that the forgiving person is touched with divinity.

A good Christian counselor must have an individual goal for the counselee that is not necessarily expressed. Crabb (1977) asserts, the Christian counselor must make the pursuit of the fruits of the spirit his or her top priority (Gal. 5:22,23). I strive for all those fruits in my own life and feel very confident that I have made tremendous strides. In my opinion every Christian should have something to strive for, and the fruits of the spirit would be the perfect goal. I have come to understand that a Christian can be in physical pain but still be at peace with oneself and with God.

The scripture teaches that great peace have they that love the law and nothing shall offend them (Ps. 119:165). I believe that every created human being deserves to have this peace. Christian counseling is one of the vehicles to guide men and women to discover and find this peace for themselves. This peace is the foundation on which the other fruits of the spirit are laid. This peace can be achieved only with a change of heart, and only God through the regenerating power of the Holy Spirit can initiate that change. People need Christian counseling today than ever before in their lives.

Sin is in the heart of man. It depresses him and causes him to think negatively and in deficit motivation. Crabb (1977) asserts, Christian counseling must aim to change the counselee to expression motivation by understanding that it is not events that change our feelings but the mental evaluation of the events that affect how we feel. There is a conscious and an unconscious mind residence in each person. People talk to themselves every day and it is not a sign of insanity as some people would make you believe. It is important to understand one self. However, in order to under-stand oneself, one has to know oneself in order to spot problem from a far.

Problems develop when personal needs for survival are not met and when an individual feels a sense of insecurity. In a relationship a partner will claim to need approval from the other, but what is needed is security. People need to understand that things cannot replace people. Possessions and money may give a semblance of security but only good relationship with people can give a sense of peace and comfort. Crabb (1977), states this succinctly when he writes, "depending on material possessions for happiness is like lowering a bucket into an empty well in order to satisfy thirst.

There must be a change in thinking, attitude, and goal. Life is all about relationship. The very relation-ships that carry the potential to injury in such heinous ways, also hold the potential to restore love and trust, and eventually lead to peace (Walsh, 2009). The goal is to seek peace through change. Again, genuine change is only possible through spiritual intervention and only the Christian counselor can provide this guidance.

Change is indispensable to every successful bib-lical counseling. One of the fundamental questions that the counselor should ask the client at the appropriate time should be, are you willing to change? Regardless of what we are trying to change, change is a must if peace is to be realized. Crabb (1977) suggests, a good place to start is to identify, problem feelings. Cross' Basement Theory for Couples Conflict Resolution is a good tool to use in uncovering problem feeling. This theory will be introduced to you late in this book.

The way a person functions is inextricably bound to the way in which he or she thinks and believes. Some people focus on the past and as long as they do, change will not be possible because no one can change the past (Adams, 1973). Change cannot be achieved by force. The individual must get to the place where he or she recognizes the need for change and expresses the desire for the change. Change does not come by chance, it calls of intentional and deliberate effort. With God's help, nothing is impossible and change can be a reality.

Biblical change must be the goal of Christian counseling because change is hard. Can the Ethiopian change his skin or the leopard his spots? Then may you also do good, that are accustomed to do evil (Jer. 13:23). There is a need for Christian counseling to provide guidance in ethical and spiritual living. The task of the Christian counselor is to call for repentance, which is a call for change. A change of mind leads to a change of life. In the Christian worldview, change cannot come without divine intervention through the regenerative power of the Holy Spirit. Only a Christian counselor can provide the counsel and guide towards this end.

COUNSELING WITHOUT CONFORMING TO THE STATE LAW

The world in which Christian are called to live in is not getting any better as so many would have you believe. In fact, this world has been a proving ground to test two plans of government, God's and Satan's. Although Satan's plans have failed miserably, he continues to thrive on man's ignorance of that reality. There are laws that govern the operation of the universe because the Creator God is a God of order. Physical, natural, and moral laws were set in motion even before man was created therefore, not all laws are the result of sin.

Adam and Eve at their creation had knowledge of the original law of God, it was imprinted upon their hearts. If the law had not existed before creation Adam could not have sinned (SDA Bible Commentary, Vol.1), and Cain certainly would not have known that he had done something wrong when he killed his brother Abel (Gen.4:8). There are rules and laws that govern our conduct as Christian counselors and there are ethical guidelines to follow. There can be no true peace, satisfaction, or contentment in this world of sin without rules and laws. Every effective counselor must follow ethical and guiding principle as well as state laws. The God whom we serve is a God of order and He sets things in motion that must move in order less they collide.

PRIVILEGED COMMUNICATION

There are two laws that the clergy person must adhere to and these laws are effective in all fifty states. The two kinds of laws serve to limit, influence, or inform clergy privileged communications. "Privileged communication" refers to an immunity granted to certain individuals and professionals that exempts them from testifying in court. The first is child abuse reporting laws (CARL), which have exceptions for "spiritual healing." Child abuse reporting laws (CARL) have emerged as the prime statues limiting clergy persons privileged communications (Bullis, 1991). CARL require a broad spectrum of professionals to report suspected child abuse; they define which professionals are considered "mandatory reporters" and civil and criminal penalties are set forth for mandatory reporters who do not comply (Bullis & Mazur, 1993). Second, all religious counselors probably have a duty to protect their counselees and to protect third parties who are in danger from the counselee.

It is very important for pastoral counselors and others working for religious organizations to recognize that clergy communication is not always privileged, particularly when suspected child abuse is present. Clergy or other religious professionals are mandatory reporters if they are called upon to render aid to any child (Bullis & Muzur, 1993). It is interesting to note that all states criminalized the failure to report child abuse for mandatory reporters. Such failure can result in a misdemeanor punishment with fines, punishment and or probation, and possibly a period of mandatory education (Bullis & Muzur, 1993).

While clergy are mandatory reporters, Florida, like New Jersey, require everyone to report child abuse.

Every clergy person must take time out to inform and educate himself or herself along with their congregation concerning these laws. Ignorance on the part of the clergy person is no excuse for not adhering to the law especially, when it involves the life of a third party, the abuse of an elderly person, or a minor. If there is anyone who should adhere to this law it is the clergypersons because they have easy access to both the elderly as well as minors. More stringent laws have been passed that require everyone who has to come in contact with minors to get a background check. This is the law and religious organizations including churches are not exempt.

DUTY TO PROTECT THE THIRD PARTIES

It is not generally expected or even required for one to come to the aid of another. However, the story of the Good Samaritan sets the bar for Christian conduct (Luke 10:30-37). The counselor has a special duty and obligation to his or her counselee. It is the responsibility of the spiritual counselor to ensure that the counselee is not left stranded psychologically, emotionally, or spiritually. The laws have put in place certain relationship exceptions because to succeed in counseling there must be a relationship between the counselor and the counselee that is based on trust and mutual respect. This is similar to the physician patient-relationship and the psychotherapist-client relationship.

Some counselors argue that counselees will not fully divulge their thoughts to the counselors if they knew that the counselor must warn others. This they say would undermine the value of therapy. On the horns of this dilemma, the Tarasoff court stated that when therapist, using the standards of their profession, determine that their counselee poses a danger or threat to someone else, the therapist is required to use reasonable care to protect others (Bullis & Muzur, 1993). Christian counselors should have no problem adhering to this principle, if indeed they are born again.

Religious organizations must incorporate this level of training and sensitivity to all who avail themselves for a ministry that involves counseling. Society has become more litigious and counseling is one of the vulnerable areas of the church's operation. Designated professionals are required to warn third parties where counselees threaten physical violence against "reasonably identifiable" third person (Bullis & Muzur, 1993).

Although the clergy person has certain protection and exemptions, there are still a few grey areas that can leave a clergy person vulnerable to litigation.

There is still an open question as to whether third parties should receive less protection from religious counselors than is expected from secular counselors. At least one author, from a legal standpoint, has advocated that, requiring clergy to protect third parties is unmanageable if not unwarranted (Milne,1986). Milne (1986) suggests, because clergy has no universally accepted code of ethics or doctrine and enjoy broad privileged communications and First Amendment protections, clergy are unique and different from other counseling professions.

Christian counselors should be the ones to raise the bar to a higher standard than secular counselors by doing what it takes to protect life at all cost. This may mean that all pastors who conduct counseling at any level should seek some form of license. Unfortunately, some clergy persons do take advantage of their parishioners and counselees under the guise of counsel. The first rule of ethics in any helping profession, especially the counseling profession that serves human needs is: do no harm. Those who continue to disregard this important ethical rule, will be dealt with by the law of the land and by God himself. It is a woeful situation when Christians have to lose faith in their clergy persons because of unethical and unchristian conduct.

LEGAL ISSUES AND PROFESSIONAL MALPRACTICE

We are living in an increasingly litigious culture and society. There are scores of unforeseen legal issues and avenues for professional malpractice that are propping up in churches. Lesbians, gays, bisexual, and transgendered persons present their own unique concerns for clergy and Christian counselors. There is a move by some states to level the counseling field by providing license to pastoral counselors as well as other mental health professional. Religious counselors must not state expressly, definitively, or evenly imply that they are "pastoral counselors" unless they have been licensed.

There are many, even without basic theological training who take on the title of pastor. This pastoral designation brings with it certain counseling expectations. It must be made clear that a clergy person who counsels is different from a clergy person who presents himself as a licensed counselor. There are legal arguments for a clergy person not to pursue licensure. (1) Religious counselors do not need licensure to conduct counseling within the parameters of their congregation. (2) Religious counselors are safe as long as they do not represent themselves as possessing counseling credentials they do not have. (3) Most states specify that their licensing laws do not apply to religious counselors.

Essentially, each state clearly defines the counseling activities that counselors may legally conduct. Religious counselors need to consult their specific state's statutes for such specific regulations and requirements because state-regulated titles are not the same as designations from professional organizations. Being a member of a professional organization does not give the right to use the professional designation, example "pastoral counselor" while being a member of the American Association of Pastoral Counselors. The pastor must be academically and professionally prepared to function as a pastoral counselor and recognized as such by a licensing body.

It is of vital importance for pastoral counselors to familiarize themselves with the state licensure laws because some of the practices and actions taken even in a religious setting can be called into question. According to Bullis and Muzur (1993), there are four fundamental reasons for clergy persons to be familiar with the state licensure laws. The first, states specifically, regulate, under certain circumstances, the counseling performed by religious counselors. Second, religious counselors need to be precise when they describe their counseling services or attribute to themselves titles or qualifications that may be reserved only for those who have been licensed. Third, both clergy and nonclergy who work for religious or spiritual institutions may erroneously assume that their work is shielded from state regulation, when in fact their work is construed as counseling. As such, it falls within state regulation for purposes of assessing criminal acts, trade name violations, and civil suits. Fourth, courts may draw an important distinction between religious counselors who are state licensed to perform counseling and those who are not for purposes of privileged communication. This means that certain professional groups are exempted, within certain parameter.

TRANSFERENCE AND
COUNTERTRANSFERENCE

Inherent in counseling is the problem of transference and countertransference. Christian counselors must be conscious of these realities and do everything to guard against them. Transference and countertransference are Freudian terms for the dynamic in therapy during which feelings are transferred, or redirected, from one person to another (Yale, 2013). One of the rules in Christian counseling is to do no harm. According to (Clinton et al., 2005), one of the mistakes some counselors make in the process of counseling is to engage in excessive self-disclosure and transparency. Extreme openness can move the focus of the counseling session off the client unto the counselor. This unwise approach does harm to the client and is an injustice to the counseling process. This ultimately can lead the client to experience transference.

A counseling or therapeutic relationship has failed when the counselor and the client have incompatible personalities and transference or counter-transference issues occur that cannot be resolved by the counselor. Transference and counter-transference issues generally surround sexual attraction. Once there is a slight detection of this, it is time for the counselor to make a referral. Referrals are also in order when the counselor recognizes that the counselee's need is beyond his or her scope of practice or when consultation is inappropriate, unavailable, or unsuccessful (Clinton et al., 2005). A referral source should be presented to the client and the client should be given the opportunity to choose. As much as possible, counsellors referred to shall honor prior commitments between client and referring counselor or church (Clinton et al, 2005).

In today's religious world many pastors end up hurting their parishioners by providing counsel which is above their training and skillset. Collins (1988) asserts, sometimes we help counselees most by referring them to someone else whose training, expertise and availability can be of special assistance. In order for this to succeed, pastoral counselors must engage in peer reviews within the scope of a professional association. The responsible and caring counselor should be acquainted with the work of the counselor to whom the counselee is being referred.

SEXUAL MISCONDUCT

Since there is zero tolerance for sexual harassment and misconduct in corporate America, it should never be tolerated in ministry or among Christian counselors. Does this mean that, corporate America's standard has become the church's standard, absolutely not! The standard for the church is always based on the Word of God and Christian counseling is based on scripture. In 1 Corinthians 7, Paul gives the biblical foundation for sex which is confined to marriage and forms the principles in marriage. Anything that is done sexually outside of these guiding principles should be considered sexual misconduct.

Sexual misconduct is not sexual ignorance and the Christian counselor needs to have some understanding of the biology of sex. Sexual misconduct is a violation of Christian ethics and principles. There will be time when the pastoral counselor will need to devote some counseling time to what constitute sexual misconduct. The rules and laws have changed and a certain look on the opposite sex can be construed as sexual harassment. The moral elasticity of our postmodern and post-Christian culture has crept into the church and has affected it (Clinton et al., 2005).

Many church leaders and pastors are losing the battle of moral purity and ethical standard through sexual misconduct. Many who are engaged in the pastoral ministry seem to forget that they should not be engaged in any behavior that is harmful to themselves or others. This is not so much a denominational problem as it is personal. Clergypersons must strive to be an example to the believers and this includes the relationship they have with their creator God. Paul's counsel to young Timothy is for all clergypersons today whether young or old (1 Timothy 4:12).

There is an ethical code of conduct that governs every primary counseling discipline. A code of ethics is a systematic statement of ethical standards that represent the moral convictions and guide the practice behavior of a group (Clinton et al., 2005). Every serious Christian counselor must familiarize himself or herself with the code of ethics that governs Christian counseling. This code of ethics covers parishioner control through pulpit exploitation, printed hyperbole, the abuse of conferred power, and sexual misconduct (Clinton et al., 2005). The church and its mission are brought into disrepute and its message unduly compromised by sexual misconduct of pastors and other denominational workers.

Sexual misconduct is criminalized in almost every state and it is unethical. It includes every kind of sexual exploitation, deception, manipulation, abuse, harassment, relations where the sexual involvement is invited, and relations where informed consent presumably exists (Clinton et al., 2005). Sexual misconduct and forbidden sexual activities include, but are not limited to, direct sexual touch or contact. According to Clinton et al., (2005) sexual misconduct also include: seductive sexual speech or non-verbal behavior; solicitation of sexual or romantic relations; erotic contact or behavior as a response to sexual invitation or seductive behavior of counselees; unnecessary questioning and or excessive probing into the counselee's sexual history and practices; inappropriate counselor's disclosure of client's attractiveness, and sexual opinions.

The worse thing that can happen to a counselee is to be harmed and sexually exploited by a counselor. A counselor who is expected to uphold the ethical rule to "do no harm" and protect the counselee. A counselor who is supposed to be guided by Christian standards and principles. One may ask, why would a Christian counselor or a pastor stoops so low? The undisputable answer is that the devil will go to any length to destroy a prospective candidate for heaven. If Satan were to succeed in allowing people to lose faith in Christian counselors, he would strike a major blow to the helping profession.

If Satan were allowed to have his way and to succeed in his ploy to manipulate the minds of men, there would be no difference between Christian counselors and secular counselors. God would not allow this to happen so we know that Christian counseling will thrive. This is one of the reasons why Christian counselors need to enter into spiritual, physical, and psychological self-care. Christian counselors are not indestructible nor sin proof. They need to enter into self- introspection and self-reflection mode almost on a daily basis. They have to pray for victory for themselves as much as they do for their counselees, because Satan is the arch deceiver.

Satan seeks to counterfeit everything that God has created and declared to be good, and anything that God makes, Satan hates. Satan's ultimate goal is to deceive and destroy everything that is good. Christian counseling is very relevant today and if it is rightly utilized, it can help to stabilize the Christian Faith. Satan is already in charge of many church pulpits and he dictates what is being preached from them. Many churches today no longer believe in a literal heaven or a literal hell, when the scriptures teach otherwise. I choose not to name any of them here, but they are out there.

Regardless of the Devil's scheming and apparent manipulation, truth will always prevail in the end. There is absolute truth and Christ Himself declares that He is the way the truth and the life (John 14:6). The Christian community knows how the story will end and that gives the faithful hope to endure. Anyone who subtracts from the word of God will miss heaven (Rev. 22:19, 20). For these reasons, Christian counseling continues to be very relevant today and is in great demand.

Every well establish organization or denomination should have a sexual ethics committee. There should be written guidelines and procedures that govern the working policy of the denomination. A sexual misconduct handbook should be made available to every employee and the same should be reviewed annually.

This annual review helps to keep employees alert to its importance. It is also important for a local congregation to be educated concerning sexual misconduct because many times the victim is a member. When dealing with sexual misconduct, the pastoral counselor must know and understand when to use the following terms: accuser, accused, victim, perpetrator, bias, prejudice, and predisposed

THE NEED FOR PROFESSIONAL TRAINING

Christian counseling is very relevant and is in greater need today than ever before. There is a thin line between morality and ethics and the Christian counselor needs to be practical, ethical, and morally sound as he or she provides counsel. There is therefore, a need for clergy person in general but Christian counselors in specific to become more ethically informed and professionally prepared for the multiplicity of problems that one encounters in counseling. It calls for much discipline and measured constraint for Christian counselors to practice only within the boundaries of their competence. The temptation to do otherwise is always lurking around the corner and many have fallen victims.

Practicing within the boundaries of one's competence is Standard Practice number 17 in the American Counseling Association Standards of Practice. Coming at number 18 in the Standards of Practice is continuing education. Seldom is continuing education a requirement among clergy persons, even within the confines of their own religious organization. However, Christian counselors are expected to stay current and relevant. Therefore, they must engage in continuing education in order to maintain their professional competence even if it is not a requirement by their employing organization.

Pastoral counselors and all those who seek to embrace the discipline of counseling must strive towards professional competence. Based on their education, training, and professional credentials, many pastors today are practicing outside the boundaries of their competence. Providing general counsel to a parishioner is like an unwritten rule in most churches, and professional training in counseling is not a prerequisite to undertake such counseling. According to Clinton et al. (2005) many pastors also embrace this expectation to the point of being overconfident with their abilities to perform. Life and counseling for that matter, are so complex, so full of mystery that overconfident assurance can be just as wrong, just as toxic for your patients as ignorance and lack of confidence (Clinton et al., 2005).

The Christian counselor must also recognize that, like the clergy person, his or her job is not just a profession but a calling. A calling that should be motivated by a love for people and a willingness to serve. Counseling, as a profession, usually attracts kind and noble persons. Healthy motivators for one pursuing a career in counseling, or a lay counseling ministry, include the desire to help others and a perceived "calling" that is confirmed by a body of Christian believers (Clinton et al., 2005). The Christian counselor must have a love for God, a zeal for God's glory and a love for fallen humanity.

There is a need for Christian counseling because people are coming into the church who are overwhelmed with the cares of this life brought on by sin and its consequences. Some are flooded with distresses like father absence, abuse, violence, marital discord, and emotional problems, Clinton, et al (2005). People get depressed because of sin and there is only one answer for the sin problem. Jesus is still the answer to the human dilemma and the solution to the sin problem.

The Christian counselor must present Christ to the counselee as the sin pardoning savior who loves the sinner unconditionally.

According to Sanders (1997), therapists and Christian counselors continue to wrestle with situations in which honoring one ethical principle (like confidentiality) may result in violating another (for instance, someone may be physically harmed unless the therapist breaches confidentiality). This presents a serious ethical dilemma for therapists and Christian counselors. In a world in which Christians and Christian minded people are not immune to fickle mindedness, a Christian counselor needs to be mentally, psychologically, and spiritually prepared to deal with the changes in mood, mind, and desires that can impact the counseling outcome. This is often encountered in marital counseling and even the courts have reemphasized the fact that marriage counseling is a regular part of a clergy person's job (Bullis &Muzur, 1993). This of course, includes pre-marital counseling.

BIBLICAL FOUNDATION FOR CHRISTIAN COUNSELING

Biblical foundation for Christian counseling does not begins with scripture, but with you the counselor. You must communicate to the counselee that you genuinely care and really want to help. According to Powlison (2003), the most common misunderstanding of "biblical counseling" is the notion that quoting Bible verses is the defining methodological feature. It is necessary and important to bring God's word to the center and impress upon counselees its inestimable value. But quoting scripture as the defining, is limited only to the Bible believing person. The Christian counselor must take the individual from where they are to where God wants them to be.

In Christian counseling Jesus is our model and example (1Peter 2:21, John 13:15). He took time out to counsel with unbelievers but it was always in the capacity of teaching them. Therefore, there is room for the Christian counselor to have a didactic conversation with an unbeliever. The counselor must see with biblical eyes and intend with spiritual intention (Powlison, 2003). The general worldview must see Jesus Christ as savior and Lord and as the only one that can pardon and forgive sin, the root cause of man's problems. This is a distinctive feature of Christian counseling that sets it apart from all others.

The Biblical foundation for Christian counseling begins with prayer. The counselor should prepare for counseling largely by prayer for himself and for his counselees (Adams, 1973). This is strikingly different from what the psychotherapists do because secular psychology is built on humanism. Humanism is a doctrine which fervently insists that man is the highest being, the central event in all history. Everything revolves around man and is evaluated in terms of its advantages to man (Crabb, 1977). While there is a germ of truth in that reality, man was created by God, he is a creature and not creator (Gen. 1:26-27). Ultimately, man must answer to God and can never be God.

The Book of James 5:16 clearly states, prayer of the righteous man is especially helpful to the sinning member. Prayer itself may be the essential element of the counseling process and ought to be offered at least at the close of the session (Adams, 1973). The value of prayer should never be underestimated. Walsh (2009) states succinctly, prayer is not necessarily an appeal to God, nor is it merely asking another source to do something for us. Prayer is an opportunity to go inside ourselves, alone or in community, and call upon our own desire and resources to create change.

Prayer is communication with God because he is the only one to whom prayer should be addressed. A paradigm shift has begun to take place in the helping profession as it relates to spirituality. There is a steady integration of spirituality taking place in clinical practice. The general public has expressed a need for mental health and health care professionals to attend to the spiritual dimension of their lives (Walsh, 2009). Over eighty percent of survey respondents preferred to have their own spiritual practices and beliefs integrated into any counseling process and seventy five percent wanted physicians and therapists to address spiritual issues as part of their care (Walsh, 2009).

Biblical counseling is about change and all true change must begin from the inside. God is the only one who can initiate and bring real change. True Christian counseling is built upon a biblical understanding of people (Creation), problem (Fall), and solutions (Redemption). It focuses upon the process of sanctification, growing to reflect increasingly the relational, rational, volitional, and emotional image of Christ (Clinton et al., 2005). Like the scripture, Christian counseling is a gift to the Christian from God therefore, it cannot fit into the mold of secular counseling and psychology. The integrationists will continue to have problems in trying to integrate the two disciplines, although there are areas where they sometimes overlap. Abraham Maslow's classical need hierarchy is one such area that overlaps.

The main features in Maslow's theory is that people in general are not generally motivated to meet their "higher" needs until their "lower" needs are met. This means that people can stay at one stage of their lives if they do not get the right motivation to move on. The five human needs in Moslow's list beginning with the most basic are:

1. Physical - Such as food, water, and heat from the cold, etc. These are elements necessary to maintain physical life.
2. Security – Meaning physical security.
3. Love – This could be emotional security
4. Purpose – Significance and worth.

5. Self-actualization – This is the expression of the highest form of humanness. This is having the capacity and determination to develop oneself into a full, creative, and self-expressing person.

Notice that possession is not mention because a person can achieve the highest, self-actualization, without being rich or wealthy. Every child of God has the capacity and opportunity to achieve self-actualization. According to Crabb (1977) the first four needs are essentially self-centered. They involve a taking in, rather than a giving out. Interestingly, the self-actualization, the ultimate and highest need in Moslow's theory comes close to the biblical concept of becoming mature in Christ, developing our spiritual gifts and expressing our God given worth in freely worshipping God and serving others (Crabb, 1977).

THE EFFECTIVE PASTORAL COUNSELOR

The Christian counselor is not just another professional, he is a caregiver and a shepherd. His first care must be meted out to himself. JoAnn Zerwelch (2006) suggests, "only through deliberate self-care are we able to be strong enough, grounded enough, to confront the fears and sufferings of patients and families." Christian counseling is about caregiving and Josey (2015) asserts, "anyone who finds himself or herself in the helping and caring profession must understand that there is no room for mediocracy." It is important to understand that spiritual pain is real. Maxwell (1990) states, "unresolved spiritual pain can negatively impact physical healing."

The effective pastoral counselor will seek to have a measure of balance in his or her own life. There must be balance among those who are striving for the pastor's time, attention, and counsel. This balance is not automatic, the counselor must create it and be consistent in its execution. The pastor must create this balance as he or she build an understanding relationship among the parishioners. The balance comes with boundaries, limitations, and with the understanding that the pastor is just one person. Essential to this balance is the pastoral counselor's personal devotional life and family time.

The pastoral counselor's family should come first at all times. Most professionals fall in this area and the clergy person is no exception. Nevertheless, effective pastoral counseling begins with the pastor's family.

This is fundamental and foundational because if the pastor's family is not together, everything that come from the pulpit would be under a dark cloud. The worse feeling that any parishioner can have of a pastor is the feeling that the pastor is hypocritical and insincere. Those seeds are generally sown directly or indirectly by the pastor's family and family-life. The story of the sons of Eli the priest illuminates this thought (1Samuel 2:12-17, 27-36).

The effective pastoral counselor will seek to know his congregation and seek out spiritual gifts. Everybody has the capacity and ability to help somebody. According to Crabb (1977), every Christian is called to a ministry of helping others, especially those of the household of faith. Crabb points out that there are three kinds of counseling ministries: (1) Encouragement is one kind of counseling ministry available to every Christian, (2) Responsibility to teach biblical principles as do pastors, elders, and other church leaders, and (3) Specialized ministry of counseling involving deeper exploration into stubborn problems (Crabb, 1977).

The effective pastoral counselor's life must be a committed life of service geared to please God in everything. In Hebrews 13:15,16, we are told that believers have two responsibilities, (1) to offer the sacrifice of worship to God and (2) to offer the sacrifice of service to others. It means therefore, if I want to please God and to be in God's favor, I must be keen on my worship and service. Christian counselors assist their fellow believers to grow and mature in Christ and in their relationship with other people (Clinton et al., 2005). Service to humanity is really the best work of life, but this service must be unselfish and carried out God's way. Such counseling also provides Christians with an opportunity to represent Christ in a therapeutic encounter with unbelievers (Clinton et al., 2005).

CHRISTIAN PATIENT AND FAMILY COUNSELING

Church members Christianity and spirituality do not make them immune to the ill, woes, and sicknesses of this present life. Christians also experience and have their different thorns in the flesh as the Apostle Paul experienced (2 Cor. 12:7). If this is a factual statement, then every church needs someone or a team of people who can provide service to the sick and shut-ins and their families in general. Many Christian seniors have fear and trepidation as they face the reality of leaving their homes to go to an assisted living facility or even a nursing home. Some of these Seniors experience a sense of neglect and ultimate abandonment.

They dread the day when they lose their independence and become patients in a facility. When that day does come however, it is comforting to know that the church to which they belong would continue to minister to them. This should be an ongoing dialogue every church and the best person to facilitate this conversation is the pastor. Many Christian elderly end up making no decision or poor decision when it comes to placement and treatment because there is no on-going communication on the subject. This is generally seen in the African American communities and churches.

Every church needs to have a well establish ministry for the seniors. People are living longer and therefore, the number of elderly persons in our society has grown dramatically in recent years. Retirement states like Florida and Arizona are seeing many who have retired at 65-67 years seeking employment at places like Walmart and in the case of Florida, Publix Supermarket chain. The is a reality because of the high quality of our healthcare, improved standards of living, and the technological advancement that has impacted the industry. The elderly are faithful church goers and financial supporters. There is hardly any church that can survive financially without them.

The concerns and ministry to the elder cannot go unnoticed. They need to be carefully and professionally monitored because the onset of dementia that goes undetected can result in fatality for an elderly person who still drives. The license could have just been renewed prior to the dementia diagnosis. These elderly persons find it extremely difficult to give up their keys to their vehicles. This represents a part of who they are and it means giving up their independence. This is where family counseling becomes invaluable because its not just the elderly who is now a patient, but the family as well. The elderly as well as family members need to be prepared for the imminent decline in physical and cognitive functioning.

TREATING THE SICK WITH RESPECT

An invaluable part of pastoral counseling is providing spiritual care for the sick with love and respect. Every pastor should strive to become a caregiver, not just to care for a congregation in a church setting but more so to visit the members when they are sick. Pastors who are not trained in this area most times, also forget the ones who are caring for the sick. True care-giving does not end with the sick person, the patient, but extends to the family members as well. The pastor visiting the sick must be alert to senses of seeing, hearing, and smelling. Much can be learned by active listening, keen observation, and unusual smell.

Sometime after the visit with the sick is over, the pastor should spend some quality time with the care-giver or the family. This is not so much time to provide counsel but rather to listen. Everyone has a story and the pastor or caregiver who is able to ask the right questions, can get the patient or family member to share their story. This can be truly therapeutic for the patient and family member. A very tired and stressed caregiver cannot provide quality care and may be in need of personal care also. I have known of instances where the caregiving spouse passes and leaves the patient behind.

The pastoral counselor cannot approach the sick like the doctor or the nurse. Physicians and nurses are socialized by colleagues and mentors to become detached from the humanity of those suffering. Medical students learn to redefine human problems as depersonalized biomedical puzzles, Zerwekh (2006). The pastoral counselor and caregiver cannot approach the sick and dying with such dehumanizing tendencies. The pastoral counselor at this point in time is representing Christ not just to the sick and dying but to the nurse and family members who are present. The scripture teaches that nothing is impossible with God therefore, dramatic and miraculous healing is always a possibility.

The pastoral counselor must know how to approach the sick with a terminal prognosis because some people of faith still fear death. When the sickness is serious but not terminal, the pastoral caregiver should inquire before the visit to the patient's room because at this point the very prayer will be different. There is always hope in the air and that must not be taken for granted. Sometimes the prognosis may be terminal and is accepted by the patient, but some close family members may not be ready to let go. Here again, the pastoral counselor's ministry goes beyond the sick. In a room packed with family members, the pastoral counselor is not just ministering to the sick, but to all the family members present in the room.

According to Zerwekh (2006), the caregiver must understand the different types of death awareness in order to guide the patient and family in finding meaningful growth and reconciliation. This is very important because the open awareness mentally and psychologically prepares the family for the inevitable. Closed awareness prevents any choice of end -of-life planning for the patient and makes reconciliation with family and friends impossible (Zerwekh, 2006). When there is respect and trust through a caring relationship between pastoral counselor and the patient's family, it becomes easier to divulge delicate information.

Zerwekh in her book, introduces the ministry of caring presence and explains how important it is for the caregiver to let go of self and deliberately focus on the other person as a human being (Zerwekh, 2006). This is transformative and when fully understood can build a relationship bridge between the sick and the pastoral caregiver. The ministry of presence becomes more meaningful to the patient. The concept of the "I-Thou" relationship as opposed to the "I-It" relationship is foundational in the practice of Caring Presence (Zerwekh, 2006).

The foundation work of Elizabeth Kubler-Ross' Five Stages of Grief Process is a must read for every pastoral caregiver because from this point on, this knowledge would be needed to effectively minister to the family. These are: denial, anger, depression, bargaining, and acceptance. Zerwekh (2006) states, grief can be summarized in a wide range of bodily complaints such as appetite change, disturbed sleep, exhaustion, trembling, shortness of breath, to name a few. The one that is particular damaging to the bereaved is called "ruminative coping." To ruminate is to chew over and over. The cow is a ruminant animal because it chews its cud.

THE PASTOR AS A CHAPLAIN

Every pastor needs to have some knowledge of chaplaincy. They should be encouraged by their denominations to seek training in Clinical Pastoral Education (CPE). At least one unit of CPE should become a requirement for ministry. This is important because the quality and content of the CPE training prepares the pastoral counselor to minister to the elderly church member with professional know how. The pastoral counselor can help the elderly parishioner as well as family members to identify causes for reversable confusion and allay fears of family members that something more serious might be amiss. Of course, this level of ministry is not limited to the aged but to all ages.

The pastors who are also train in clinical pastoral education, upon retirement from the rigors of pastoral ministry, can continue to provide spiritual care in a hospital or hospice environment. These environments are less stressful and as pastoral caregivers they can provide quality care because they have the pastoral ministry experience. It is also a plus for the retired pastor to avoid boredom while earning. More importantly, the training will provide the added skill in hospital, nursing homes, and hospice visitations. There is a definite need for pastors to be trained with hospital and bedside skill and this comes with the chaplaincy training.

The training will help the pastoral counselor to develop a sharp eye, an acute ear, and a keen sense of smell. All these senses must be engaged when a visit to the elderly is made, because proper communication of need can improve the patient's quality of life. This is all the more important if the elderly is still living alone. There are signs and symptoms due to the loss of oxygen due to medical conditions such as respiratory disease, heart disease, hypothermia, hypertension, and anemia. An early recognition or detection of any one of these signs can result in saving a life. These things are not taught in the seminaries of today to regular ministerial students. They are only exposed to the care of the sick when a course is taken in chaplaincy.

An alert and knowledgeable pastoral counselor can detect certain symptoms and help to save the life of the elderly by summoning for medical assistance. Competent medical care can often alleviate such conditions and peace and assurance to the elderly person. If a hospice professional is not present, a knowledgeable pastoral counselor can recognize the eminency of death and prepare the family to meet the inevitable and initiate anticipatory grief. My experience has taught me that early preparation can be cost effective. However, in some cultures there is a barrier to pre-arrangement due to cultural beliefs. Therefore, cultural awareness is important even when one is trying to help.

Some parishioners can be stubborn when it comes to seeking medical help and counsel. A gentle conversation can help them to recognize their need to see a doctor or need for treatment for reversable problems. The informed pastoral counselor must not overlook the family member who is the caregiver. Sometimes an impatient and frustrated family member will communicate harsh judgement to those struggling with diminished capacities. The dignity and value of the sick elderly person must be respected and maintained at all times. It becomes the pastoral counselor's responsibility to provide counsel to such family members. Elderly abuse is considered a crime and there are many ways an elderly can be abused. The pastoral counselor should be the intermediary for the sick and the family caregiver.

MINISTERING TO THE FAMILY

The pastoral counselor's ministry does not stop with the visit to the elderly. Although some family members or immediate care giver may belong to another denomination, the pastoral counselor can still provide professional support without disrespecting their faith tradition. The Jehovah's Witness would be offended if you were to invite them to pray with you. Ministering to the family is not limited to the spiritual only. According to Zerwekh (2006), caregiving does not end with the patient but extends to the family members as well.

Everyone has a story and the pastoral counselor, nurse, chaplain, or caregiver who is able to ask the right questions can get the patient or family member to share their story. Narrative, in fact, is the way we live, the way we reveal ourselves and understand the story of our lives (Clinton et al., 2005). The pastoral caregiver who visits occasionally needs to hear their story also. Telling their story can almost be like a sacred ritual because of the relief it brings in sharing. This can be truly therapeutic for the patient or family member who embraces the opportunity to share their story. Remember, narrative, and especially relationship narrative, is the way God tells us His story in the Bible (Clinton et al., 2005).

The informed pastoral caregiver should know about the services that the local hospice organization provides and be willing to make the suggestion to the sick or family member. Most primary care physicians would normally make such referral but sometime that referral is made very late due to professional bias or selfishness. Who suffers but the elderly patient who is denied the comfort and care that is available. There are times also when a patient dies enroute to the hospice house because of a late referral by a primary care doctor or hospital care team.

As the pastoral counselor ministers to the caregiver, moments of stress or tiredness might be detected. This should not go unnoticed and every effort should be made to provide help for the caregiver. Sometimes the caregiver could be a spouse, a son or daughter, a relative, or a friend. If the patient is with the hospice care, arrangements can be made with the local hospice to provide respite care for the patient so that the caregiver can have a few days off. This would most definitely be appreciated and could bridge the gap to further dialogue with the family. Unfortunately, most pastors are not aware of these services and provisions that can help to alleviate caregivers stress.

In the case of a diagnosis that gives the individual six months or less to live, the pastoral counselor needs to provide reconciliation counseling and closure. There may be someone with whom the sick person may need to speak with to find peace and comfort. The pastoral counselor should be able to guide the patient and facilitate this intervention for reconciliation and healing. There are times when it is not possible for a face to face appearance or contact due to time and distance. At such time, the pastoral counselor can initiate communication through a telephone call. It is important to do all the ethical and spiritual things possible to provide comfort for the dying person. Not with-standing, it can also be a relief on the part of the family member and helps to facilitate closure in the event of death.

Chapter 4

Conflict Resolution

Conflict in a relationship as intimate as marriage is unavoidable because marriage is never between identical twins. The differences in personalities and characters will invariably spawn conflict. This also means that anywhere two people are there is a potential for conflict. The emphatic and undisputable reality is that all couples have conflicts. Therefore, conflict should never become the issue and should never be the cause for separation and divorce for a Christian couple.

The society we live in today has evolved into a symptom management society. This is generally seen in the physical and mental health care industries. It has now made its way into the psychological and counseling fields. What we need is the ability to diagnose and treat root cause. Cross' Basement Theory for Couples

Conflict Resolution (CBTCCR) seeks to bridge the gap between symptom treatment and treating root cause for couples in conflict.

Not all conflicts can be resolved, some will have to be managed. A conflict can be healthy and can create a fertile environment for growth between the couple. According to Crabb (1977), effective counseling is centrally and critically a relationship between people who care. Worthington (1999), recognized conflicting couples as those who regularly fight over issues without arriving at a mutually acceptable resolution. In order to eliminate this fight, counseling is necessary. Christian couples are not immune to conflict and if they are not taught how to handle it when it shows up, their marriage also can become a statistic.

Effective counseling is built on a relationship of trust between the client and the counselor. Counseling is not a discipline like dentistry or medicine which depends fundamentally upon a growing amount of technical knowledge administered by highly trained professionals. According to Crabb (1977), effective counseling is centrally and critically a relationship between people who care. Professional and pastoral counselors alike tend to rely on a few techniques and two or three basic principles, perhaps without ever clearly thinking through exactly why their counseling efforts should work, Crabb (1977). Cross' Basement Theory for Couples Conflict Resolution is one such instrument that can be used as a diagnostic tool in couple's conflict.

Donald Richardson's book about couples in conflict, deals heavily on family systems theory and how it impacts conflict and the counseling processes and phases. The book challenges the counselor to adapt a theory and strive to perfect its use in his or her counseling practice, Richardson (2010). Interestingly, Richardson did not use the word theory to mean a hunch. He alluded to Dr. Murray Bowen who used the term as a scientist would, as a formal statement as how things work, Richardson (2010). It is advisable to learn about Bowen's Family Systems Theory and understand the family as an emotional unit. With the understanding of the family as an emotional unit, the perceived individual problem is not really seen as individual, but a part of a larger whole, the family.

Life is all about relationship and in general there are only two types of relationships. The vertical relationship between mankind and God and the horizontal relationship between mankind and his fellowmen. Hope-focused Marriage Counseling by Everett L. Worthington Jr. and Couples in Conflict by Ronald W. Richardson are the recommended books to be used with Cross' Basement Theory. Like other forms of counseling, these books are based on good relationship and Worthington's book provide the perfect guide to Brief Therapy. The main thesis of his book is the strengthening of marriages and reducing of divorce through spiritual interventions and motivation of couples in strengthening their resolve to wait on God's work in their marriage, (Worthington, 1999).

WHAT IS CROSS' BASEMENT THEORY?

Cross' Basement Theory is a diagnostic instrument that can be used in pre-marital and marital counseling to unmask potential problem areas for pre-marital couples in counseling and also diagnose the primary cause of conflict between married couples. Interestingly, doctors would not administer treatment or write a prescription without first checking the patient and doing a thorough assessment. Through tests and assessments, a proper diagnosis is made. Sometime, the nature of the test result may necessitate a consultation with a specialist.

The society in which we live today has evolved into a symptom management society. This is generally seen in the physical and mental health care industries. It has now made its way into the psychological and counseling fields. Many types of sicknesses are unduly prolonged while others end in deaths, because health care professionals end up treating symptoms rather than root cause. While conflict in a relationship as delicate as marriage is expected, there is always a root cause to every conflict. A marriage stands a better chance of surviving if the couple knows the cause of their constant quarreling and fighting.

What we need is the ability to diagnose and treat root causes. Cross' Basement Theory for Couples Conflict Resolution (CBTCCR), seeks to bridge the gap between symptom treatment and treating root causes of couples in conflict. In the medical field a proper diagnosis must be made before corrective treatment can be administered. Similarly, counselors should not begin counsel based on the intake information only or on the counselees declaration of why they are seeking counsel. An assessment, as is customary the case, does not reveal the root cause of a conflict in most cases. Sometimes it takes several sessions before the hurting parties begin to open up and reveal their inner pain.

When an individual in excruciating abdominal pain visits the doctor, many times the complaint that the patient makes has nothing to do with the sickness he or she is experiencing. Unfortunately, many patients die because an improper diagnosis was made that results in the wrong treatment being administered. Many stories are told of patients who died hours or a few days after visiting their primary care physicians. Lives are saved after thorough patient assessments are done using interviews, tests, and diagnostic instruments to arrive at the correct diagnoses.

Cross' Basement Theory of Couples Conflict Resolution is a diagnostic instrument that is capable of diagnosing the real source of a couple's problem or area of conflict. This instrument, correctly administered, honestly executed, and rightly interpreted, is capable of revealing the couples' potential areas of conflict or current conflict. The instrument is capable of pinpointing or diagnosing areas of conflict among couples who have been married for one to ninety-nine years. The instrument also works well in pre-marital counseling in helping couples discover the area or areas in their relationship that has the potential for conflict.

When a proper diagnosis is made, the pastoral counselor or therapist is then able to tailor his or her counseling to provide solution to the specific problem in the couple's relationship. This is the essence of Brief Therapy and solution focused marriage counseling that the Basement Theory embraces. In this instance, the old adage makes it clear. To be forewarned, is to be forearmed and prevention is better than cure. A correct diagnosis also limits the number of counseling session needed to get the couple back on track. Therefore, Solution Focused Brief Therapy is the main model chosen for counseling interventions with Cross' Basement Theory. It focuses on solution and hope for the couple in counseling.

The foundation for the Basement Theory is love and hope. Love is a central value in every relationship and marriage that has hopeful aspirations. According to Worthington, Hope-focused marriage counseling deals with people's beliefs and values within the context of solving the marital problems so that the couple will be more loving (Worthington, 1999). Love cannot thrive in an atmosphere of bitterness, resentment, and disrespect. People's hope, belief, and values are all part of the solution process.

DOES THE BASEMENT THEORY WORK IN ANY CULTURE?

Conflict is not gender or culture specific. Anywhere two people are, there is the potential for conflict. Therefore, CBTCCR is a conflict resolution instrument that can be used in any culture and with any couple regardless of age. The success of the instrument is based entirely on the honesty of the couple and their ability to execute the requirements of the instrument. While the instrument can be used effectively in any language or culture, and by anyone, it was specifically designed for the Christian community and Christian counseling.

God created human beings in His own image and the reflection of God's image continues in all people regardless of age, sex, skin color, or moral condition. A child does not become human because he or she begins to assimilate the cultural patterns of an environment. Rather, the child is human by virtue of God's creative act (Gen. 1:26-27), Grunlan (1983). This reality leads us to understand that because of the Adamic sin, each child is born with the natural propensities and proclivities to sin. Sin therefore, is an inescapable reality due to the original sin.

The sin problem cannot be corrected without the word of God and divine intervention. Sin deforms humanity in more ways than just the physical. Therefore, there is need for healing. The literal meaning of healing is becoming whole. For the psychiatrist Carl Jung (1933,1958), wholeness includes the sacred dimension, which is at the heart of healing (Walsh, 2009). Healing is a process that we are all involved in at all times. Sometimes people heal physically and they don't heal emotionally, mentally, or spiritually. Sometimes they heal emotionally but not physically (Remen, 1993). Whether physical, emotional, mental, or spiritual; all true healing comes from God.

The Christian counselor knows that there is a biblical solution to every problem. He or she knows also that Jesus was tested, "in all points as we are" and He successfully met every temptation without sinning (Matt. 4:1-10). There is no cultural barrier to God's power to set men and women free from sin. It is the task of the Christian counselor to understand your problem, help you to discover God's solution to it, and to encourage you to do what God requires you to do about it (Adams, 1973). This also establishes the relevance of Christian counseling today.

The Christian counselor cannot turn just to the theories of men to find solution to the problems of life. Without a clear understanding of how problems develop, counseling can become nothing more than a warm, friendly conversation full of good intentions (Crabb, 1997). The counselor must create a healing environment by laying the proper foundation for honest communication to remove the pain caused by sin. According to Walsh (2009), the ultimate desired outcome is to create a healing environment for family members that relieves their suffering from illness experiences.

If there is anything that must be maintained at all cost, it is the integrity of the Scriptures as the authoritative standard for Christian counseling (Adams, 1973). The Christian counselor must keep in mind that the basic need of people is to be born again or regenerated. Once this experience has been theirs, they need to be instructed towards Christ-centeredness in all their living (Kent, Sr.1974). This can only be accomplished by a man or woman of faith who has also experienced hope. This also helps to establish the relevance and the need for Christian counseling today. The Bible is a Textbook for pastors and Christian counselors (2 Tim. 3:16,17).

Without hope, the Christian counselor cannot communicate the hope and encouragement that many counselees need (Adams, 1973). People, regardless of their culture, creed or nation, need hope. God instilled hope in Adam just after the fall (Genesis 3:15) because like Adam, sin has worked its defeating and disheartening effects in all our lives. According to Adams (1973), there are times when every Christian is dispirited. Hope and love must be the unwritten recurring theme in every counseling session. Hope helps to give zest to life as one faces each day with optimistic expectancy.

WHICH THERAPY WORKS BEST WITH THE BASEMENT THEORY

There are many different therapies and counseling interventions that are used to impact counseling today. However, the therapies that work best with CBTCCR are: Solution Focused Brief Therapy, Cognitive Behavioral Therapy, and Couples Therapy. Each of these therapies will be briefly highlighted. The Christian counselor and therapist must understand that there is no one size fits all in counseling therefore, other theories of interventions can be explored.

Solution-focused Brief Therapy (SFBT) is concerned with an individual present and future as well as the individual's goals. It is a goal-oriented therapy that places little or no emphasis on past experiences or circumstances. Therefore, the issues that brought a couple to counseling are generally not targeted. The issue that brought the patient to the doctor may not be the root cause of the illness. SFBT is not confined to Couples Therapy, it works well also with individual and family therapies.

Cognitive-behavioral therapy (CBT) is a psycho-social intervention that is the most widely used evidence-based practice for improving mental health. Guided by empirical research, CBT focuses on the development of personal coping strategies that target solving current problems and changing unhelpful patterns Cognitive behavioral therapy - Wikipedia. Like SFBT, CBT is also a goal-oriented psychotherapy that takes a practical approach to problem solving and conflict resolution. It is also short-term in its interventions and scope.

Couples Therapy (CT) is a branch of the general Family Therapy. Couples Therapy can be a great help to couples experiencing difficulty in their marriage. Couples Therapy is also a good intervention in pre-marital counseling and therefore works well in the Basement Theory. Couples Therapy is a needed intervention in couples counseling and should be considered a safe choice in general couples counseling. The Christian religion is confronted with serious marital issues and conflict and caring for and nurturing couple cannot be like an annual physical examination. Couples Therapy has to be integrated into a pastor's pulpiteering and teaching. There is a need for Christian counseling today.

THE INSTRUMENT AND ITS
INTERPRETATION

Setting up the appointment is very important to the successful completion of the process. Whether the counselor or the in-take secretary takes the call, it is important to adhere to the following on the telephone: (1) Stick to the in-take questionnaire once the caller establishes the reason for the call, (2) share with the prospective counselee the available counseling slots and confirm a date, (3) discuss cost, payment option, and method of payment, and (4) Stress the importance of being on time. Richardson (2010) suggests that the counselor should never allow the first contact with the counselee over the phone to become a counseling session. The counseling session begins in the office.

The couple should be welcomed by the counselor or his or her assistant. Assessment is an ongoing process and it begins from the couple enters the office. They would be lead to the counseling room or office where they would be given instructions as to how to complete the instrument. The instructions include a commitment to honesty, no communication between them while working on the instrument, and follow the instructional guidelines on the instrument. After the couple has spent 10-15 minutes completing the instrument, the counselor enters the room, collects the completed instrument and explains how the interpretation will be done.

To begin the interpretation, it is recommended that the counselor or pastor opens up the session with prayer. This prayer is very important and should include God as the creator of the marriage institution and Satan as the destroyer of everything that's good. The couple's names should also be mentioned in the prayer and an invitation for the Holy Spirit to take control and direct the session should be made. This prayer should set the atmosphere for a spiritual encounter and re-establish the fact that couple is in the presence of the Holy Spirit to be guided by a Christian counselor.

After the prayer, the counselor would inform the couple that he or she is a Christian counselor who uses the scripture as the foundation for counseling. Jay Adams asserts that Satan has launched an attack upon God's Word. In counseling, this fact has been more than evident; it has been glaring. Within the church the sufficiency of Scripture (God's written Word) has been challenged, Adams (1979). It is very important for the couple to perceive the counselor as being spiritually connected to begin the counseling relationship.

At this point each party is handed a bible that is pre-marked at 1 Corinthians 13. It is important to pre-marked this chapter rather than to assume that the couple can find it on their own. The couple is then asked to read alternate verses slowly, but both are to read the last verse together. This is followed by a brief over-view of Solution Focused Brief Therapy as the coun-seling model and intervention of choice. Notice that up to this point, the couple that comes for counseling has not been asked any specific question concerning their marriage. By this time, the couple should be more relaxed, more informed about the counseling process, and more trusting of the counselor. It is important to build a relationship of trust between the counselees and the counselor. Those few moments help to build that relationship and relax the couple.

The counselor then turns to each and asked, why are you here and what is it that you want to come out of this session? The reason for this compound question is to sensitize the couple to the reality that every counseling session should have a goal and an expected outcome. This question helps the couple to set the goal or goals and lay the foundation to begin their solution focused encounter. It is the responsibility of the counselor to keep in front of the couple their goal and expected outcome as the session progresses. It is easy to lose sight of the goal in counseling because of heightened tension and expressed frustration between the couple. The set goals should be practical and achievable and every effort should be made by the counselor to guide the couple in achieving those goals.

Ordering your priority is the foundation on which the Basement Theory is built. People are different and consequently will also have different priorities in life. Selfishness and lack of spiritual guidance can cause one to have misplaced priorities. It only takes one misplaced priority to create a serious conflict in a marriage. It is important therefore, to have one's priorities straight.

ORDERING YOUR PRIORITY
PLEASE LIST THE FOLLOWING ON THE LEFT IN ORDER OF **YOUR** PRIORITY ON THE RIGHT: PHIL. 4:13

Name:
Age:
Marital Status:
Telephone #:

1. RELIGION/CHURCH.................1.
2. LOVE............................2.
3. GOD............................3.
4. HOUSE ....4.
5. MARRIAGE ....5.
6. CHILDREN........................6.
7. EDUCATION/SCHOOL ....7.
8. SEX ....8.
9. COMMUNICATION...................9.
10. FAMILY TIME ....10.
11. MONEY/SAVINGS..................11.
12. CAR............................12.
13. IN-LAWS........................13.
14. FRIENDS........................14.
15. WORK/JOB.......................15.

The Basement Theory was designed for couples counseling in general, but specifically for Christian counselors. It must be made clear that there is a difference between pastoral counseling as a profession and pastors who do counseling. The essence of Christian counseling, as are all things Christian, is hidden in the person of Christ as is chronicled in Col. 1:26-27 (Clinton, et al., 2005). Christ is the ultimate caregiver and the Apostle Paul counsels us to follow his example as he follows the example of Christ (1 Cor. 11:1). The church is being challenged by Christ Himself and Christian counseling is called to serve it in all its varieties (Clinton, et al., 2005).

The Basement Theory is a straight forward diagnostic instrument that can be used by all pastors in any religion. It is used specifically to diagnosed the cause of conflict between married couples and pinpoint potential areas of conflict in premarital counseling. This diagnostic instrument is not a diagnostic assessment nor is it Theory-Based Assessment. According to Sperry (2012) a diagnostic assessment is a focused assessment of the client and the current and developmental context influencing the client. The Basement Theory reveals the root cause of a couple's conflict and opens a window into the way the couple was socialized and what influences their decision making.

It is the responsibility of the pastor to seek professional training in order to provide the needed counseling to meet the diagnostic results of the instrument. According to Richardson (2010), ongoing supervision is essential to being a consistently good counselor. Simply being a good pastor or a caring person is not enough. Today's pulpits need pastors who are sensitive to the mental, physical, social, and marital struggles that a congregation undergoes. Counseling cannot be confined to the office alone. The church at worship on any given day can be transformed into a large therapy session. The pastor can address any of the identified subjects on mental health, physical health, or marital well-being.

It is imperative that pastors know their limitations when it comes to pastoral counseling. It is irresponsible and unethical not to have training and supervision in place if pastors want to provide regular counseling to their parishioners, Richardson (2010). Cross' Basement Theory for Couples Conflict Resolution (CBTCCR) is a tremendous breakthrough for Christian counselors who normally have to spend hours in different counseling sessions before getting to the root of the problem. Our prayer is for this instrument to be made available to all pastors and for them to grasp the concept, so that they can effectively employ it in their counseling ministries to their parishioners.

Counseling can be more effective when it is approached from a coaching stand point. Counseling on the one hand can become superficial, mechanical, and has a punctiliar effect after the counselees leave the office. Coaching on the other hand is more personal and has a linear effect that continues after the counselees leave the office and is conducive to faster healing. After the coaching is over, the burden is on the counselees to go home and continue to practice on their own. According to Richardson (2010) coaching takes the focus off the counselor/counselee relationship. It makes it clear that the game (figuratively speaking) is out there, elsewhere in the counselee's life. This is one of the reasons why homework is important.

The counselor (coach) is needed because he or she helps to release the tension in an emotionally charged relationship. Richardson states that the tension within a two-person system can be resolved when in the presence of a third person (the counselor) who does not take sides, stays in equal contact with both parties, tracks with them their emotional process, and leaves responsibility for their thinking and behavior with them (Richardson, 2010). A good counselor (coach) will provide the counselee with the necessary tools to work with while at home.

THE SPECIFIC INTERPRETATION: SETTING THE AGENDA

The counselor looks at both completed instruments and note how the couple list their priorities using the given list. If the male list God as his number one priority and the female list God as her number one priority, there is no potential conflict with their belief or acceptance of God as being sovereign. However, if the male places God at number one and the female puts God at number four, this would be considered a red flag and consequently a possible area of conflict or future conflict. If the female places God at number three instead of four, this would be considered the safe zone with the least possibility for conflict.

If the female places love at number five and the male puts love at number two, this is a Red Flag. The counselor should then find out what the male has at his number five and where the female places that same thing. The interpretation results in the couple setting their own counseling agenda according to the number of Red Flags in the completion of the instrument. A proper interpretation is necessary in order to arrive at a correct diagnosis.

It must be noted that each Red Flag is a subject for counsel because it reveals a present or future conflict. While it is prudent and necessary to provide general counsel, the instrument reveals the areas in the lives of the couple where there are conflicts or has the potential for conflicts. The solution focused counselor or therapist must now give priority to these revealed areas of conflict or potential conflict. This is the time to ask searching question of the couple and activate the Basement Theory. This gives the advantage of providing specific counsel and make the entire counseling experience solution focused. It is possible that no red flag shows up. In such a case, the counselor should highly commend the couple and explain the reason why there is no red flag. The counselor at this juncture would listen to the stories of the counselee in order to understand their individual premise and their individual problem.

If one of the Red Flags is about finance, the counselor has the responsibility to ask specific questions to uncover the identified problem area. The counselor would then select the appropriate questions for a pre-marital couple or a married couple in conflict. Such questions may include but not limited to the following which were adapted from Clinton & Trent (2009):

1. What is your current financial situation?
2. Do you have student loan, and if yes, how much do you owe?
3. Have you both discuss this along with other debt you are carrying into the marriage?
4. What do you consider to be the cause of your financial concern or crisis today? (The counselor should ask, do you both agree that this is the source of the problem?)
5. What do you think needs to happen for the concern to go away or to get out of this crisis?
6. How is this financial concern or crisis affecting your marriage and family?

7. How are you both currently coping with the situation?

8. Who usually handles the bill in your home? Describe the process for handling your monthly financial commitments.

9. What is the shortfall in what you need to meet those commitments? In what area can you peel back and save some money? Do you both think you can commit to tightening your belts for a while?

10. What lifestyle changes do you need to make to keep a financial crisis such as this from happening again?

11. Have you commit this situation to prayer?

12. Do you trust God to see you through this crisis?

13. Are you both willing to start praying together about this problem?

14. Are you willing to start praying right now, right here?

It is possible that no red flag shows up. In such a case, the counselor should highly commend the couple and explain the reason why there is no red flag. The counselor at this juncture would listen to the stories of the counselee in order to understand their individual premise and their individual problem. No red flag means no basement issue. It is also possible to have no red flag if the couple is not being honest in completing the instrument.

CHAPTER 5

PRE-MARITAL AND POST-MARITAL COUNSELING

*P*re-marital counseling is generally sought after and is a recommended intervention for those contemplating marriage. Christian counselors should never join two people together in marriage without engaging them in pre-marital counseling. Marriage is a gift from God and 1 Corinthians 13 is God's instruction to every couple. It would be in the best interest of every couple to memorize this chapter and put God's counsel in practice because a successful marriage does not just happen. While the word success can be considered relative to each individual or couple, a successful marriage involves a husband and wife working harmonious together towards a common goal.

A good marriage calls for pre-marital preparation because most couples spend more time planning and preparing for the wedding as opposed to demasking and getting to know each other. Some potential married couples make the mistake thinking that cohabitation will reveal their compatibility or incompatibility. As a result, they resort to shacking-up and pretending to be married. This does not just negatively affect their prospect for marriage, but it has a lasting moral, social, and spiritual effect on their lives and on the lives of their children should children result from such cohabitation.

Every prospective couple should be told that after the wedding, the marriage begins. The preparation for a successful marriage begins with honest communication between the parties according to the principles recorded in Ephesians 4: 25-32. If more prospective husbands and wives were encouraged to work on the problems of communication from the beginning of their marriages, fewer would need instruction later on at crisis period, Adams (1973).

Pre-marital counseling is geared to help the prospective couple to successfully navigate the many twists and turns that will come up in a marriage. Cohabitation lessens considerably, the chances of a successful marriage. Most people do not seek counsel before cohabitation therefore, they enter into conflict without any guidelines of how to manage or resolve this inevitable intruder called conflict. Honest and respectful communication that holds the key to marital bliss can end in a cul-de-sac, because the cohabitating couple did not take the time to receive counsel against these pitfalls. The general assumption however, is that Christians would take the principled and spiritual approach by rejecting cohabitation and embracing pre-marital counseling.

Pre-marital counseling for a Christian couple should not end without sessions on love, faith, hope, and forgiveness. Worthington (1999) suggests, the counselor should promote love, faith, and work to help the couple or individual which will help the couple with marital problems solve those problems. Sin is real and it is the only cause of problem in the world. However, sin does not occur in a vacuum, it occurs as a result of how people were socialized and impacts their cultures, values, and priorities in life. Christian married couples must understand these realities and they are best relayed through properly structured pre-marital counseling with the Basement Theory.

The fact that a couple is in love and is excited about the prospects of becoming husband and wife, does not shield them from sin and human errors. There is always habits, attitudes, and cultural proclivities to contend with that can trigger a serious problem for a marriage. The Basement Theory is geared to uncover such problems. Counseling should be provided geared towards dealing with such problems when they develop. The counsel can also be geared towards avoiding such problem. Living models can be used to demonstrate successful marriages, with the understanding that successful does not mean perfect.

The Christian church and Christian marriages are in a dilemma because of the lack of models. The Church needs to give a platform and a voice to those whose marriages have aged and have experienced scorching summers and shivering winters. These couples can share the love, commitment, and discipline that kept them together. According to Adams (1973), modeling is an essential biblical method for teaching. Modeling should not be confined to marriage but every aspect of Christian living (2 Thessalonians 3:6-15). The apostle Paul was single but he taught the concept of Christian modeling the life that counts (Philippians 4:9). Example is always more powerful that precept and a sermon lived is more effective than a sermon preached.

The Bible is still the fundamental guide for Christians contemplating marriage. The scripture provides one basic and fundamental guiding principle- a prohibition against sexual intercourse before marriage (1 Cor. 6:9-20; 7:1-9; Gal. 5:19-21; and Eph. 5:3). In order to succeed in this respect Christian couples contemplating marriage must seek counsel to protect themselves against social and emotional issues that the scripture does not address. Touching and kissing can lead to sexual stimulation which involves caressing the genitals and fondling the breast (Grunlan, 1983). Young couples need to be aware of these potential pitfalls that can affect their marital relationship.

Post-marital counseling is an idea that I would like to introduce in the counseling arena. Couples who complete their pre-marital counseling should commit themselves to return six months after their wedding to go through the post-marital counseling. Like a new vehicle, the dealership recommends that the new vehicle receives service after certain miles are driven or time has lapsed. Similarly, the new couple may develop early problems in their marriage and because of pride, they refuse to seek counsel early. This conflict will not disappear, but over time gets worse.

The post-marital counseling session serves to remove that feeling of pride that an early return for counseling might create. Their return for counseling should be based on a prior signed contract and memorandum of understanding. A counselor should not be surprised if a spouse were to call in to arrange for an earlier post-marital visit before six months. This in reality is highly possible because conflict can erupt even on the honeymoon. The post-marital counseling session provides the perfect occasion for the counselor to ask all the right questions that should keep the couple on track, or if they went off track, get them back on course.

Sometimes, an individual is able to mask a behavior in such a way that it becomes undetectable during pre-marital counseling. Here again, if this couple did not receive an intervention using the Basement Theory, this counseling intervention stands a good chance of unmasking this problem. The questions that will be asked by the counselor would be based upon the diagnosed problem resulting from the Basement Theory. The following counseling intervention is based on the concept of the post-marital counseling with the pastoral counselor who conducted the pre-marital counseling with the couple.

Based on the pre-marital counseling the couple received, the counselor would begin the post-marital session as follows:

1. Ask how was the drive coming over? Get the couple to respond to something that they need not think about in order to respond. The purpose of this is create a relaxing atmosphere, because chances are, they could be having early problems and had an argument on their way to the counseling office.

2. Thank them for coming and open up the session with prayer. The prayer should be specific to their visit and mentions God who has the answer to every question and the solution to every problem. It is strongly recommended that they be given another diagnostic exercise using Cross' Basement Theory for Couples Conflict Resolution (CBTCCR). This second exercise should be compared to the first to be used only as reference by the counselor.

3. Remind the couple about the process, whereby each one should show respect by listening without interrupting the other. It is important to lay down some ground rules for how you (the counselor) plan to proceed with the session. The question should then be asked, so, who will go first in sharing with me your six months progress and growth? This is a time where the counselor takes notes while maintaining eye contact with both parties. The tone of voice, posture, and general body language are important to listen to and observe at this point. Expect the best after six months but never take it for granted that all is well.

   After listening to the other party, the counselor may seek to congratulate them on the marital progress and growth they have made as a couple or change course to address the problems or concerns they have raised. At this time, the counselor can share comparatively the result of the second diagnostic exercise.

4. Depending on the outcome of their respective sharing, the counselor should have the following practical and spiritual questions ready:

a. How are you both doing spiritually?

b. How do you feel about your relationship with God at this point?

c. Do you plan to make any lifestyle change?

d. What is your current financial situation?

e. Are you practicing Christian benevolence and are you tithing?

f. Who was chosen to handle the bills?

g. What is your short-term goal and what is your long-term goal?

h. Are you praying together and have you seen an answer to any of your prayers?

i. What new have you learned about each other?

j. If you could make one request of your spouse, what would that be?

5. There should be no expected return visit after a post-marital session however, couple uncovers problems that must be addressed before the counselor, additional session should be arranged before they leave the office. A regular post-marital session should not go beyond two hours.

SAVING AND SPENDING STRATEGIES FOR PRE-MARITAL AND MARITAL COUNSELING

The scripture teaches that there is a way that seems right unto a man, but the end thereof are the ways of death, Proverbs 14:12, 16:25. It is so easy for marriage and family to be torn apart by poor and unwise financial management. Money does matter. It represents more than just a medium of exchange. According to Grunlan (2013), money represents power, love, status, and many other things such as security, confirmation of one's worth, and opportunities for one's self and one's family.

In the New Testament Jesus speaks more about money than heaven and hell combined. The basic concern of the Bible seems to be with man's attitude towards money. While we are counsel and cautioned not to love money because the love of money is the root of all evil (1Timothy 6:10), it is wise to understand how to use it, whether you have little or much. Finance is major cause of problems in a marriage. That is why two people, contemplating marriage and becoming a couple, need to explore this topic of money in depth (Grunlan,1983).

Here is a successful money management formula that any family can use to achieve balance, mutual respect, and a respectable and secured future for your family. This approach can only work if husband and wife are willing to combine their salaries and decide to work together as partners. This calls for love, trust, respect, and teamwork all wrapped in a package of open communication.

A marriage is like a business in which the husband and wife are in fact partners. For this marriage and partnership to be successful, goals must be set and an annual audit or stock taking is made each year or as needed. The annual audit is important to ensure that the family is on track to achieve their goal or do they need to change something. Follow these eight steps and enjoy the blessings of the Lord.

1. Appoint a business manager: Decide who would be responsible to pay the bills when they become due and keep the partnership in equilibrium.

2. Make a budget: Green (1978) suggests at least four purposes or values of budgeting for

couples. He points out that a budget (1) maximizes income, (2) provides a realistic view of financial status, (3) opens communication, (4) reduces tension. It allows a couple to invest in those things they value most.

3. Open three separate accounts under the following headings: (a) Family's savings account, (b) Family's expense checking account, and (c) Family's personal account.

A. The Family's Savings Account

In this account the family places all the family's savings (excluding mutual fund, IRA, Annuity, etc.). This account includes down payment for you first house, life threatening emergency spending, down payment or to purchase a new car, and college education. A pledge should be made between the couple that under no circumstances other than what is designated should these funds be used. The use of any of these funds, ever for the designated items, should be with mutual understanding.

The Eye-opening Family Scenario

Jim and Mary have been married for four years and have a two-year-old son Timmy. They have established their three accounts for success and budget to save twenty thousand dollars ($20,000) in five years, in order to make a down payment towards the purchase of their first home. They presently have sixteen thousand five hundred ($16500) saved towards this goal and have begun to look around for a community of choice, since they would reach their saving target in a few months.

One eventful day Jim received a call from his brother Joe who told him that he needed five thousand dollars in two days, if not he would be going to prison. He explained that this was a life and death situation and Jim was his last resort. After Joe's sycophantic begging and pleading, Jim told him that he would have to go home and speak with his wife and get back with him that night. What if Mary were to refuse and hold out that their savings was only going to be used as designated. Jim would be faced with a dilemma by having to go back to his brother and say no, he cannot help.

This in turn would trigger the problem of ill feeling between Joe and Mary because Jim had already given the impression that the money was available but he had to speak with Mary first. This approach by Jim inadvertently created a family rift and possible bitterness and resentment that could take years to heal or overcome. What might have been a better approach? Could there be a better response to Joe's request that would lead to a better outcome regardless? Absolutely! Pay close attention and read inductively.

This is the correct response and the winning approach to the same scenario:

Jim listens to Joe's begging and pleading with interest mingled with measured scolding and counsel. He told Joe that he did not have any money and he was sure that his wife Mary did not have any either. Certainly, he did not lie to his brother because the money saved does not belong to him nor his wife, it's the family's money. When Jim got home he related the story and the request from his brother to Mary.

Mary listened sympathetically and felt very sorry for Joe. Mary then turn to Jim and stated emphatically, Jim we cannot allow Joe to go to prison. He has been a good brother and uncle to our son. Jim interrupted and said he agreed, but how were they supposed to help when they have no money to meet Joe's need. Mary suggested that they push back their house purchase to the following year or make a smaller down payment and take the money from their family's savings. This was a huge sacrifice but they both were in agreement that they would use the money from their Family's savings to help Joe.

Later that evening Jim called Joe and told him that he went home and told Mary about his situation and need. He told Joe that Mary was determine that they should find the money and help because he was a good brother and uncle to little Timmy. Jim told Joe that the money was coming from the down payment for their home and he had Mary to thank for it. What has this approach wrought? Firstly, it galvanized the family relationship between the brothers. Secondly, it provides a greater possibility for repayment because it is not perceived so much as coming from brother Jim but from Mary. Thirdly, it creates not only a deeper bond with Mary but also heightened respect for her. Lastly, if Joe was a jerk and a scammer and had no intention of paying back the money, this couple would have had every reason to refuse help to him should a future need arise and he would prove himself to be unconscionable if he were to approach them again.

B. The Family's Expense Account
   This second account must be a checking account and is used expressly for the payment of the family's bills. It serves as an operating expense account and is managed and executed according to the budget. This is the account the couple's salaries are paid into and from which all other accounts are serviced and maintained by the business manager. While both names are on this account, only the family business manager uses it. The other party must know what to do in the event that the business manager for any reason become incapacitated or is not available to service the account. There should be planned time for the family to discuss the family's expense account. Some families may choose to do this quarterly, half-yearly, or annually. This account is the heartbeat of the family liquidity. It is like the bucket that draws water from a well. It

must always have a cord that is long enough to reach to the bottom of the well should the water lever falls. The business manager must so manage that the expense account is never in the negative.

C. The Couple's Personal Spending Account
The family's budget must show how much the couple needs to spend as individuals. This expenditure should include but not limited to: Travel, lunch, and possibly an amount for miscellaneous. Please bear in mind that the couple at this point must see themselves as a team working to achieve a specific goal and to please their creator God in all that they do. The scripture teaches that the two have become one therefore, they must now do things together. At the end of each year the couple may choose to roll over their personal accounts balances into the family's savings account. God expects families to work together in an honest and dignified way and this can only be accomplished

when there is respect for the Divine authority found in scripture.

According to Jay Adams (1973), there is need for divine authority in counseling and only biblical counseling possess such authority. The Basement Theory is based on scripture and follows the example of Jesus, the Christ who did not have return visits after his counseling or spiritual encounters with people. The story of the Samaritan woman in John 4:4-26 provides the best example of one such counseling encounter with Jesus. Jesus met the individual once and the work of transformation takes place.

According to Kent, Sr. (1974), one of the greatest needs of mankind is peace with God. If he has peace, many of his problems will vanish. The Lord Jesus Christ is the answer to this need, and only the individual with the Christian message can proclaim the supply of this need. This is the supreme advantage that the Christian counselor has over all others (Kent, Sr.,1974). The scripture teaches that, "great peace have they which love thy law and nothing shall offend them" (Psalm 119:165) and blessed are the peacemakers for the shall be called the children of God (Matt. 5:9).

The aim of the Basement Theory is to meet with couples experiencing marital conflicts and diagnose the sources and root causes of their conflicts and problems. After a diagnosis is made, spiritual counseling is provided that is solution focused and specific to the diagnosed problems. The instrument will invariably reveal that the conflict is triggered by an unfulfilled need. According to Crabb (1977), because humans are both physical beings and personal beings, they have both physical needs and personal needs.

These unmet needs are generally the source or triggers for conflict. It is the responsibility of the pastoral counselor who understands and knows how to interpret the Basement Theory to defrock the problem and point the couple towards the solution. Two hours per session are generally recommended to spend with a couple from problem diagnosis to counseling intervention and homework. The nature of the diagnosed problems and resulting conflicts may require follow-up sessions using brief therapeutic interventions.

The solution does not reside in the office of the pastoral counselor therefore, homework assignment will be necessary for most couples. Although the assignment does not necessitate the return of the couple to see the pastoral counselor, it is highly recommended that they return to ensure that the assignment is done. This visit should be scheduled by the pastoral counselor before the couple leaves the office. After the second visit which includes the sharing of homework assignments, all subsequent visits become the couple's sole prerogative.

While the couple is not expected to return, they will continue their work at home after being provided with the tools to continue on the path to relationship and marital wholeness. One of the purposes of the homework is for counselees to develop problem resolution and coping skills on their own. This is the primary reason why Solution Focused Brief Therapy is one of the counseling intervention models chosen for the Basement Theory. The recommendation is that the pastoral counselor ends the session with both parties holding hands and praying for each other. According to Adams (1973), the Christian minister and counselor must be willing to assume the full task of ministering to men and women who suffer from the pains and miseries that stem from personal sins.

The pastoral counselors should be careful not to create a situation in which the counselees feel totally dependent on them. One of the purposes of the homework is for counselees to develop problem resolution and coping skills on their own. Homework helps them to work through certain problems and conflicts through love, forgiveness, and reconciliation. Homework helps them to develop the ability to do things together.

Every married couple will need to understand the concept and value of love in confession, forgiveness, and reconciliation. Solution focused as opposed to problem focused, is the biblical approach to marital problems. It is impossible for two people to live together without having some areas of disagreement and misunderstanding. According to Grunlan (1983), there are five categories of differences between couples. These categories are taste, habits, values, thinking, and temperament. Therefore, a categorical diagnosis is necessary to arrive at the root cause.

After the diagnosis is made and the root cause of the problem is identified, it is time for the counselor to listen to the couple as they take their own time to tell their stories. The good pastoral counselor will listen carefully as the burdened ones tell their stories. Careful notes must be taken and interruption should be made only to seek clarification. Telling their stories is not merely for sharing information, but this is also therapeutic in nature. Sometimes, one or both parties may end up crying. It is always a good thing for the counselor to recognize the intensity of the pain and the level of hurt at this time and pause to offer specific prayer for the couple.

In the spirit of prayer and by the guidance of the Holy Spirit, the pastoral counselor must seek to point out difficulty and show how it may be solved (Kant, Sr. 1974). While psychological problems requiring medical attention sometimes lie at the base of difficulties which counselees bring to the pastoral counselor, most of their problems issue from the fact of sin (Kant, Sr. 1974). It is generally believed and accepted that most sicknesses are a result of the mind. It is therefore, imperative that pastoral counselors know their limitations and be prepared to make the necessary referral.

HOME WORK FOR THE COUPLE

The following homework assignments are designed to help the couple to grow in love, appreciation, and acceptance of each other as children of God. This is possible only through daily communion with God and communication with each other while working together.

I. GOD'S DESIGN: In Genesis 2:18 God spoke clearly and said, "it is not good for the man to be alone."

   A. List four things you believe God means when He said, "not good" in Genesis 2:18. (example.) The creation was not complete so it was not good.

   1.

   2.

   3.

   4.

   B. Who initiate the marriage ceremony according to Genesis 2:22(b)?

   1. Who was the father of the bride?

   2. Who blessed the wedding?

   3. Who were the witnesses?

C. List three implications this should have
   on your wedding and marriage
   1.
   2.
   3.

D. Marriage is referred to as a covenant in
   Malachi 2:14.
   1. What is the meaning of the
      word covenant?

   2. What implication it has for
      your marriage?

E. Marriage is God's plan for man therefore:
   1. God can fix anything in marriage that
      goes wrong (True or False).
   2. Marriage is not a covenant, it is a
      contract (True or False).
   3. Under no circumstance should
      a Christian seek a divorce (True
      or False).

II. PURPOSE DETERMINED BY GOD

    A. Companionship

        1. Why do you think Genesis 2:19-20 come between Genesis 2:18 and verses 21-22?

        2. From Genesis 2:18, draw four conclusions from the words alone and help meet that reflect God's purpose of companionship in marriage

           a.

           b.

           c.

           d.

    B. Sexual Intimacy (Genesis 2:24-25).

        1. What is your understanding of these verses?

2. Read 1 Corinthians 7:1-5 (the use of different translations is recommended).
    What conclusions have you drawn about the frequency of sexual relations?

3. If biblical love is shared, what should be our focus in sexual behavior?

4. Why is sex not just for procreation? Give four reasons.
    a.
    b.
    c.
    d.

C. Children (Genesis 1:27-28)
    1. In light of these verses, do you think every couple should have children? (Yes, No), explain.

2. Do you think children make a marriage a marriage? (Yes, No), Explain

3. Do you think that a childless marriage is reason for divorce? (Yes, No), explain.

4. In view of Ephesians 5:22-32, what is one reason that God desires permanency in marriage?

III. PERMANENCY DESIGNED BY GOD
(Matt. 19:3-19; 1 Cor. 7:10-16;
Rom. 7:1-3; Mk. 10:1-12; Lk. 16:18.
A. What is God's pleasure regarding marriage?

B. Does God permit divorce? For what reason?

C. If divorce occurs, is forgiveness still required of the offended party? (Yes, No), explain.

IV. FUNCTIONS WITHIN MARRIAGE.

A. Husband (Ephesians 5:16-6:20; 1 Peter 3:7-9). What is your understanding of these commands?

B. In view of modernity, culture, and current laws, are these commands outdated? (Yes, No), Why?

C. With privilege comes responsibility.
List three responsibilities that comes
with headship?
1.
2.
3.

D. Since the husband is to follow the
example of Christ over his church, read
St. John 13 and describe how Jesus exer-
cised leadership.

E. List five ways you can lead your spouse
after Christ's example
1.
2.
3.
4.

COUPLES CONFLICT RESOLUTION QUESTIONNAIRE: TOWARDS RECONCILIATION

A conflict resolution questionnaire for married couples only (1 Peter 3:1, 7-12)

PLEASE ANSWER ALL QUESTIONS COMPLETELY AND TRUTHFULLY AS FAR AS YOU CAN REMEMBER.

Name_____ Date _____

No. of children _____ Age_____

Years of Marriage _____ Tel._____

1. True love is an unconditional commitment to an imperfect person   T or F

2. Love grows and anything that grows requires time   T or F

3. Anything that grows can die if it is not nurtured and fed   T or F

189

4. True love come from God   T or F

5. There can be true love without
    commitment   T or F

6. The things that you are committed
    to help to shape who you are.   T or F

7. The things you are committed to
    can help to build you or destroy you   T or F

8. In order for a marriage to succeed
    all it need is love   T or F

9. Commitment is more important than
    love in a marriage   T or F

10. We ultimately become whatever
    we are committed to   T or F

11. Wealth and Fame are the enemies
    to every marriage   T or F

12. It is ok to cheat on your spouse
    if it enhances your business   T or F

13. It is ok to cheat on you spouse if
    he or she will never find out   T or F

14. Cheating can be habit forming
    and addictive   T or F

15. Speaking the truth only makes
    the wrongdoer looks good   T or F

16. Speaking the whole truth is the
    first step in building back trust   T or F

17. It is always a sign of sincerity when
    the guilty party confesses after he or
    she is caught   T or F

18. In a marriage, it is always better to
    make sleeping dogs lie than to bring up
    past unfaithfulness that your spouse
    did not know about.   T or F

19. Protection of the guilty third person
    is always a sign of poor judgement and
    Questionable sincerity.   T or F

20. Contact with the third party after an
    unfaithfulness has occurred is a sign of
    maturity and should not be questioned
    by the faithful spouse.   T or F

21. Once forgiveness is given, the guilty
    party should be treated as if no wrong
    was Ever done.   T or F

22. Unfaithfulness in a marriage is a
    mark of disrespect but not selfishness   T or F

23. To change your life, you must change
    the way you think and sometimes the
    Friends you keep.   T or F

24. There is a thought behind everything
    we do.   T or F

25. People who say they will stop doing
    sinful acts and change are lying to
    Themselves and will repeat the
    same sin later in life. Only God can
    help the To change a sinful behavior   T or F

    2 Cor. 5:17-20 & 1 John 1:9
    (Please read and continue)

26. True repentance is Godly sorrow
    for sin and not sorry you were caught.   T or F

27. Once a person is caught they will
    forsake the sinful act and live right.   T or F

28. There can be no forgiveness without
    genuine confession.   T or F

29. True reconciliation comes after
    confession at all times.   T or F

30. Genuine forgiveness, repentance,
    and reconciliation are all divine attributes   T or F

Additional Resources to use with Cross' Basement Theory

1. Donald H. Baucom and Norman Epstein, *Cognitive Behavioral Marital Therapy (New* York: Brunner/Mazel, 1990).

2. Everett L. Worthington Jr., *Marriage Counseling: A Christian Approach to Counseling Couples* (Downers Grove, Ill: Inter Varsity Press, 1989).

3. Franklin N. Boyd, *Black Families in Therapy: Understanding the African American Experience* (New York: Guilford Press, 2006).

4. H. Norman Wright, *Marital Counseling: A Cognitive, Behavioral, & Biblical Approach* (San Francisco: Harper and Row, 1981).

5. Judson J. Swihart and Gerald C. Richardson, *Counseling in Times of Crisis* (Dallas Word Publishing).

6. Neil S. Jacobson and Andrew Christensen, *Interactive Couple Therapy: Promoting Acceptance and Change* (New York: W.W. Norton, 1996).

7. Randolph K. Sanders, *Christian Counseling Ethics: A Handbook for Therapists, Pastors*

And Counselors (Downers Grove, Ill: Inter Varsity Press, 1997).

The Basement Theory was specifically designed for couples counseling in general but specifically for Christian counselors. It must be made clear that there is a difference between pastoral counseling as a profession and pastors who do counseling. The Basement Theory is a straight forward diagnostic instrument that can be used by all pastors in any religion. It is used specifically to diagnosed the cause of conflict between married couples and pinpoint potential areas of conflict in premarital counseling. It is the responsibility of the pastor to seek professional training in order to provide the needed counseling to meet the diagnostic results of the instrument. According to Richardson (2010) ongoing supervision is essential to being a consistently good counselor. Simply being a good pastor or a caring person is not enough.

It is imperative that pastors know their limitations when it comes to pastoral counseling. It is irresponsible and unethical not to have training and supervision in place if pastors want to provide regular counseling to their parishioners (Richardson, 2010). Cross' Basement

Theory for Couples Conflict Resolution (CBTCCR) is a tremendous breakthrough for Christian counselors who normally have to spend hours in different counseling sessions before getting to the root of the problem. The Basement Theory is like the MRI and Ultrasound for marital relationships. It is like the couple's biopsy to confirm and identify the source of marital conflict. Our prayer is for this instrument to be made available to all pastors and for them to grasp the concept, so that they can effectively employ it in their counseling ministries to their parishioners.

We recommend that pastors who are married would first use the instrument on themselves with their spouses. Be true to yourselves as you order your priority list and don't be afraid of the result. Do not involve even your grown children in this activity at this time, just be prepared to have some level three communication with your spouse. Remember, there is always room for improvement and growth stops only when we die. Feel free to share your findings and discoveries with your family and church if you are so inclined. Life is all about relationship build on a foundation of love and mutual respect. May our love of God, the zeal for God's glory, and our love for fallen and broken humanity motivate us to work diligently and creatively to help others to succeed in this life and be ready for the life to come.

CHAPTER 6

CONCLUSION AND RECOMENDATION

*J*t is an undisputed reality that Christian counseling is very much relevant and remains in high demand. The goal of professional pastoral counseling is to produce stronger marriages and more stable families. The purpose of this book was not only to show that Christian counseling was still relevant but also to answer the question as to who is sitting in the pews of our churches. This book highlights the fact that the pews of our churches are filled with many different types of sicknesses apart from spiritual sickness. Unfortunately, for the most part, only the spiritual sickness is being addressed from the pulpit.

It is very important that religious organization plan for relevant continuing education course for clergy person. Such courses should include but not limited to Alzheimer's Disease Awareness, Grief and the Grief Process, Mental Health Awareness, The Caregiver and Self-nurturing, and Hospital and In-Home Visitation just to name a few. Religious organizations and pastors should be aware that presenters can be made available through their local chapter, hospitals, universities, and nursing facilities. Felt needs must be addressed in church from the pulpit and those needs are not limited to the spiritual. Some churches will boast that they are already doing these things however, they are done only in seminars and selected workshops with a small percentage of attendees. Mental health, physical health, and emotional well-being are all salvific in nature and should be given time in the pulpit (Mk. 1:21-28; 5:1-13; Lk. 4:33-37; 13:10-17). The church is not just to prepare people for heaven, but also to prepare them to live successfully on earth until the Lord returns.

The time has come for Christian clergy persons to recognize that Jesus' earthly life and ministry laid the foundation for Christian ministry around the world. Every Christian church must be involved in the ministry according to Christ Jesus revealed in Luke 4: 18-21. The pulpit must be used to help to alleviate spiritual and emotional pain, the agony of grief and loss, and the mental and physical trauma cause by the different forms of abuses and sin in general. The Christian people who go to church regularly, are ordinary people who are affected by the cares and stresses of everyday life. Many who are sitting in the pews each week are mentally and socially fractured and broken in spirit. Still they go with the singular hope that one day they will experience their miracle through faith and trust in the one in whom they believe, God.

I want to recommend Cross' Basement Theory for Couples Conflict Resolution to be used by all pastors. If it is used correctly, it can make a difference in every Christian congregation. It is the responsibility of the pastor, the shepherd of the flock to utilize the instrument to help couples in conflict. The hour glass of time for this world seemed to have already run out, we are therefore living on borrowed time. The global signs and declension are forecasting that this is not a world that is about to experience utopia. The end of this present world as we know it is fast coming to an end. The scripture teaches that when man thinks that it is peace and safety, sudden destruction will come (1 Thess. 5:1-4). It behooves us therefore, to treat each one as family and understand that life is all about relationship. Let us just love one another and care for each other and may Christian counseling continue to be relevant until the end of time.

References

Adams, Jay E. (1997). *A Theology of Christian Counseling: More Than Redemption*. Grand Rapids, Michigan: Zondervan.

Adams, Jay E. (1977). *The Christian Counselor's Manual*. Grand Rapids, Michigan: Zondervan.

Bancroft, Lundy (2002). *Why Does He Do That? Inside the Mind of Angry and Controlling Men*. New York, New York: Penguin Group.

Bertini, Kristine (2009). *Understanding and Preventing Suicide*. Westport, Connecticut: Praeger Publishers.

Bullis, R. K. (1991). *The Spitiyual Healing "Defense" in Criminal Prosecutions for Crimes Against Children*. Child Welfare, 70(5), 541-555. Table 6.1.

Bullis, R.K. & Mazur, C. S. (1993). *Legal Issues and Religious Counseling*. Louisville, Kentucky: Westminister/John Knox Press.

Capuzzi, David (2009). *Suicide Prevention in School*. Stephenson Avenue, Virginia: American Counseling Association.

Clinton, Tim, Hart, Archibald, Ohlschlager, George (2005). *Caring for People God's Way*. Nashville, Tennessee: Thomas Nelson, Inc.

Clinton, Tim & Trent, John (2009). *Marriage and Family Counseling*. Grand Rapids, Michigan: Baker Publishing Group.

Courtois, Christine A. & Ford, Julian D. (2009). *Treating Complex Traumatic Stress Disorders*. New York, New York: Guilford Press.

Crabb, Lawrence J. Jr. (1997). *Effective Biblical Counseling: A Model for Helping Caring Christians*. Grand Rapids, Michigan: Zondervan Publishing House.

DiClemente, Carlo C. (2003). *Addiction and Change: How Addictions Develop and Addicted People Recover*. New York: Guilford Press.

Efron-Potter, Roland T. (2015). *Handbook of Anger Management and Domestic Violence Offender Treatment*. New York, NY: Routledge.

Friedman, Matthew J. (2006). *Post Traumatic and Acute Stress Disorders*. Kansas City, MO: Compact Clinicals.

Gary, R. Collins (1988). *Christian Counseling: A comprehensive guide*, rev. ed. Nashville: W. Publishing Group.

Gorer, G. D. (1965). *Death, Grief, and Mourning*. New York: Doubleday.

Green, Ernest J. (1978). *Personal Relationships: An Approach to Marriage and Family*. New York: McGraw-Hill.

Grunlan, Stephen (2013). *Marriage and the Family: A Christian Perspective*. Eugene, Oregon.

Jemison, T. H. (1959). *Christian Beliefs*. Mountain View, California: Pacific Press Publishing.

Jobes, D. A. (2003). *Understanding suicide in the 21st century: Preventing suicide: The National Journal, 2, 2-4*

Johnson, Sharon L. (2003). *Therapist's Guide to Substance Abuse Intervention*. San-Diego, California: Academic Press.

Johnson, J. G., Cohen, P., Gould, M. S., Brown, J., and Brook, J. S. (2002). Childhood Adversities, inter-personal difficulties, and risk for suicide attempts during late adolescence and early adulthood. *Archieves of General Psychiatry, 59, 741-749*

Joiner, T.E. (2010). Myths about Sicide. Cambridge, MA: Harvard University Press.

Josey, Shenunda Simone (2015). *More than Medicine: What They Don't Teach You in Medical, Nursing or PA School. West Chester, Ohio.*

Kubler-Ross, E. (1969). *On death and dying*. New York: Simon & Schuster.

Maxwell, Katie (1990). *Bedside Manners: A Practical Guide for Visiting the Ill*. Grand Rapids, Michigan: Baker Publishing Group.

Miller, David & Berman, Allen L. (2011). *Child and Adolescent Suicidal Behavior*. New York, NY: Guilford Press.

Milne, T. W. (1986). *Bless Me Father, For I am About to Sin...Should clergy Counselors Have a duty to protect Third Parties?* Tulsa Law Journal, 22, 139-165.

Neimeyer, Robert A. (2012). *Techniques of Grief Therapy: Creative Practices for Counseling The Bereaved*. New York, NY: Routledge.

Otwell, Pat (2007). *A Guide to Ministering to Alzheimer's Patients and Their Families*. New York, Rutledge.

Paymor, Michael (2000). *Violent No More: Helping Men End Domestic Abuse*. Alameda, CA: Hunter House Inc., Publishers.

Perschy, Mary Kelly (2004). *Helping Teens Work Through Grief*. New York, YK: Rutledge.

Potter-Efron, Ronald T. (2015). *Handbook of Anger Management and Domestic Violence Offender Treatment*. New York & London: Routledge.

Remen, R. N. (1993). Wholeness. In B. Moyers (Ed.), *Healing and the mind*. New York: Doubleday.

Richardson, Ronald (2010). *Couples in Conflict: A Family Systems Approach to Marriage Counseling*. Minneapolis, MN: Fortress Press.

Rogers, Fuller Dalene C. & Knoenig, Harold G. (2002). *Pastoral Care for Post-Traumatic Stress* Binghamton, NY: The Haworth Pastoral Press

Sanders, Randolph K. (1984). *Christian Counseling Ethics: A Handbook for Therapists, Pastors, And Counselors*. Downers Grove, IL: Inter Varsity Press.

Simos, B. G. (1979). *A time to grieve*. New York: Family Service Association.

Sperry, Len (2012). *Spirituality in Clinical Practice*. New York: Routledge

Wagner, Barry M. (2009). *Suicidal Behavior in Children and Adolescents*. New Haven: Yale University Press.

Weaver, Andrew J., Hosenfeld, Charlene, & Koenig, Harold G. (2007). *Counseling Persons With Addiction and Compulsions: A Handbook for Clergy and other Helping Professionals*. Cleveland, OH: The Pilgrim Press.

Worden, William J. (1991). *Grief Counseling and Grief Therapy*. New York, NY: Springer Publishing Company.

Worthington, Everett L. (1999). *Hope- Focused Marriage Counseling: A Guide to Brief Therapy*. Downers Grove, IL.: InterVarsity Press.

Yale, Robyn (2013). *Counseling People with Early-Stage Alzheimer's Disease*. Baltimore: Health Professional Press.

Zerwekh, Joyce (2006). *Nursing Care at the End of Life: Palliative Care for Patients and Families*. Philadelphia, PA: F.A. Davis Company.

MEET BEVERLY STERLING-CROSS

*B*everly Sterling-Cross was born in Manchester, Jamaica and received her early education in Manchester. Beverly migrated to the United States when she was seventeen. She met and married Milton Sterling who predeceased her in 2012. The union produced two sons, Milton who is a MD and Wesley who is a professional chef.

Beverly received her professional training at Oakwood College, now Oakwood University, Miami Dade University and Atlantic Coast Theological Seminary. She served as an Early Childhood Educator for over twenty-seven years. She is a certified Early Childhood Educational Professional and holds a National Child Development Associate Credential from the State of Florida. In 2015 she was appointed a Notary Public by Governor Rick Scott for the State of Florida.

Beverly's teaching experience reached Korea, where she taught Conversational English for two years. She held different positions throughout her teaching career such as: Head Teacher and director of academics. Beverly however, has another passion apart from teaching. She wanted to serve in the Gospel Ministry and touch people's lives at a different level. She subsequently left teaching to serve in the Southeastern Conference office as receptionist and first responder. Her interpersonal relationship skill has impacted the lives of pastors and their families, principals and staff, church members, and those from the business sectors.

In 2017 she married Dr. Dolphy Cross who is a family-life educator, a psychotherapist, and a conflict resolution specialist. They immediately launched their ministry to couples and developed a conflict resolution diagnostic instrument now known as, "Cross' Basement Theory for Couples Conflict Resolution." Beverly wants to dedicate the rest of her life fulfilling her life-long dream of ministering to couples and families. She recently completed a PhD in Christian Counseling and the title of her dissertation is: The Relevance of

Christian Counseling Today. This is being published into a book for pastors and others in the caring profession. Her encouragement to you is to have faith in God and hope in the future you cannot see. She believes that the Creator God is in the business of making something out of nothing. She solicits your prayer and prays that this book with prove a blessing to you as a Christian counselor and caregiver.

CPSIA information can be obtained
at www.ICGtesting.com
Printed in the USA
FFHW011456301118
49661272-54075FF